Lord, Have Mercy

ELLEN MILLER

Lord, Have Mercy

Help and hope for moms on their last nerve

TYNDALE
MOMENTUM™

The nonfiction imprint of
Tyndale House Publishers, Inc.

Visit Tyndale online at www.tyndale.com.

Visit Tyndale Momentum online at www.tyndalemomentum.com.

TYNDALE, Tyndale Momentum, and Tyndale's quill logo are registered trademarks of Tyndale House Publishers, Inc. The Tyndale Momentum logo is a trademark of Tyndale House Publishers, Inc. Tyndale Momentum is the nonfiction imprint of Tyndale House Publishers, Inc., Carol Stream, Illinois.

Lord, Have Mercy: Help and Hope for Moms on Their Last Nerve

Designed by Julie Chen

Unless otherwise indicated, all Scripture quotations are taken from the *Holy Bible*, New Living Translation, copyright © 1996, 2004, 2015 by Tyndale House Foundation. Used by permission of Tyndale House Publishers, Inc., Carol Stream, Illinois 60188. All rights reserved.

Scripture quotations marked ESV are taken from *The Holy Bible*, English Standard Version® (ESV®), copyright © 2001 by Crossway, a publishing ministry of Good News Publishers. Used by permission. All rights reserved.

Scripture quotations marked NASB are taken from the New American Standard Bible,® copyright © 1960, 1962, 1963, 1968, 1971, 1972, 1973, 1975, 1977, 1995 by The Lockman Foundation. Used by permission.

Scripture quotations marked NIV are taken from the Holy Bible, *New International Version,*® *NIV.*® Copyright © 1973, 1978, 1984, 2011 by Biblica, Inc.® Used by permission. All rights reserved worldwide.

Scripture quotations marked NKJV are taken from the New King James Version,® copyright © 1982 by Thomas Nelson, Inc. Used by permission. All rights reserved.

For information about special discounts for bulk purchases, please contact Tyndale House Publishers at csresponse@tyndale.com or call 800-323-9400.

ISBN 978-1-4964-1937-8

Printed in the United States of America

23	22	21	20	19	18	17
7	6	5	4	3	2	1

For my children, Shauna and Scott,
who despite my naive, error-laden, shortsighted,
and often daffy parenting, grew into loving,
forgiving, beautiful human beings.

And for my stiletto-wearing, Jesus-loving mother,
who didn't break me either, God rest her soul.

Introduction

Dear Fellow Mom,

I am excited and truly humbled that you are willing to share a small amount of your precious time with me over the next ninety days.

In case you didn't read my first book, *The One Year Book of Inspiration for Girlfriends . . . Juggling Not-So-Perfect, Often-Crazy, but Gloriously Real Lives*, allow me to introduce you to my family. They have shaped me—and this book—in countless ways, and perhaps you'll see a bit of your own family in them too.

My husband, Steve, and I were married in 1990. When we met, I was divorced with two kids gifted from God: one that we lovingly joke I got stuck with (birthed), Shauna; and one I got to pick (adopt), Scott. Steve adopted both children as teenagers. Yes, that's how awesome my husband is.

Our daughter, Shauna, and son-in-law, Adam, are the parents to our only grandchild, Ava, born in 2007. Ava, like her mother, is an old soul who speaks the truth in love as few can. Both have been critical in the development of this book, and I am blessed beyond measure to be Mom and Sugar to these two girls.

Our son, Scott, was the inspiration for my first book. Missing for three and a half years as he battled an addiction to methamphetamines, Scott has graciously allowed me to share our ongoing story once again with the prayer that it might be a source of encouragement for other moms who struggle with a child who struggles. Our collective journey taught me more about the grace and love of Christ than I would have known otherwise.

Although I might be further along on this mothering journey than you, I suspect we have faced some of the same pressures. From our six-year-olds dribbling soccer balls in the kitchen (as we attempt to make dinner) to the "smack talking" of our teenage daughters, we moms often find ourselves on our last nerve. While our hectic schedules and family dynamics definitely contribute to our frazzled state, we also wear ourselves down when we neglect our own needs in order to care for everyone else's. Considering this might be your situation, I wrote this devotional to provide you support and insight in five critical areas that can offer you peace, hope, and joy—even as your three-year-old colors on the freshly painted walls.

The devotions found in the first section, "Lord, Have Mercy; Renew My Spirit," will remind you that you are beautifully and wonderfully made. But with that fabulous design comes some special-care instructions: In order to take care of others, you must *first* refresh yourself.

Let's face it. Moms worry. We worry about a looming due date on a work project, we worry about what's for dinner, and we worry when our children are out past curfew. So who has the time or brain cells to worry about the state of one's soul? I have learned the dangers of ignoring this deepest part of myself, so in "Lord, Have Mercy on My Soul," I will share with you how feeding your soul will fortify your mind and heart to deal with your family and your work.

Your family is the most important institution on earth, and there's nothing Satan wants more than to see it unravel. Whether you're a single mom or a married one, it's important to understand temptation and the ways it can destroy your life and those you love. We'll explore the best routes of exit in "Lord, Have Mercy; Get Me Out of This Mess."

Exhausted moms who are juggling too many balls can unwittingly blow their Christian witness to their family and friends. When this happens, we become all the more frustrated, aggravated, and anxious. I wrote "Lord, Have Mercy; Help Me Be Good" to enable you to find, keep, and demonstrate internal and external peace, even when the people around you are driving you nuts.

Last, I affirm and validate your commitment and conviction to raise your sweet babes—from those in diapers to those heading out the door with car keys in hand—in the most God-honoring way you can. You'll see that I am as passionate about doing that as you are in the section "Lord, Have Mercy as I Raise These Kids."

I celebrate our differences and thank you for your open mind and heart. I learned that the readers of my first devotional included women who considered their faith the most important part of their identity, as well as women who didn't think much about faith at all. They varied in age, life stage, and political inclinations. But regardless of our differences, I'm pretty sure we all have one thing in common: More than anything else, we long to raise our children to be thoughtful, generous, discerning, joyful human beings.

Mothering is not for wusses. It's best suited to heroic idealists, the ones who dream audaciously and absolutely never wave the white flag of surrender. Those who are not mothers—even our husbands—do not always understand our fierce loyalty. Because of this, I believe we need God's Word and one another to get these little rascals raised.

As we begin, I want you to know that throughout my days of writing this book . . .

> I have not stopped thanking God for you. I pray for you constantly, asking God, the glorious Father of our Lord Jesus Christ, to give you spiritual wisdom and insight so that you might grow in your knowledge of God. I pray that your hearts will be flooded with light so that you can understand the confident hope he has given to those he called—his holy people who are his rich and glorious inheritance.
>
> I also pray that you will understand the incredible greatness of God's power for us who believe him.
> **EPHESIANS 1:16-19**

Because you're short on time and those kiddos are growing faster than Johnson grass, let's get our visit under way.

For his glory,
Ellen

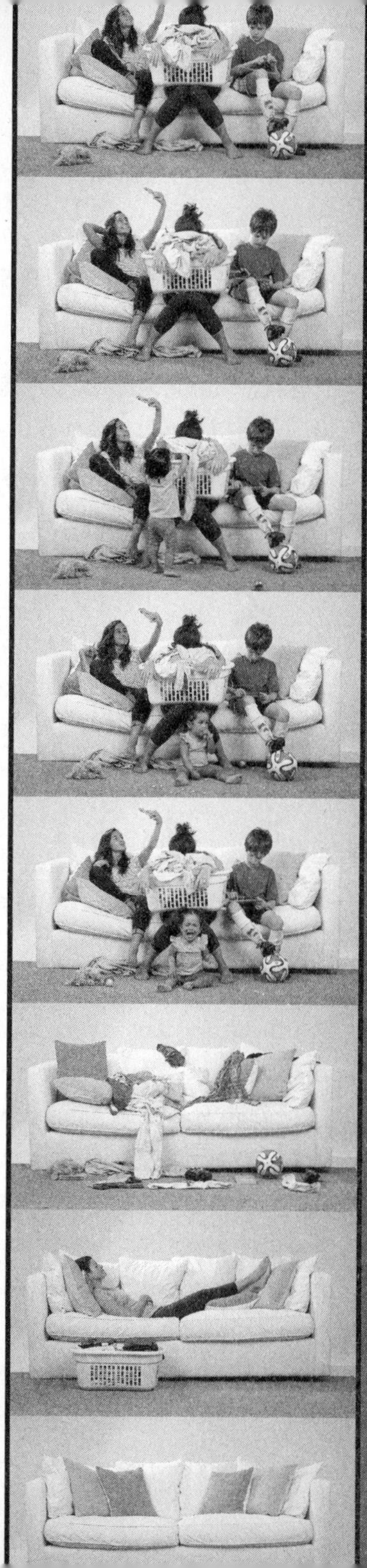

Lord, Have Mercy RENEW MY SPIRIT

SPECIAL-CARE INSTRUCTIONS

I AM A FREAK ABOUT MY CLOTHES. Oh—not so much about the brands I wear but about how they're laundered. It matters so much to me that I always read the care instructions before toting any garment to the dressing room. Weird, I know.

But here's why: I want my clothes to fit well and I want them to wear well. After too many of my garments were stretched, shrunk, or damaged at the dry cleaner, I determined that the best way to ensure their fit and longevity was to take care of them myself.

Most of my clothes have care instructions that call for washing on the gentle cycle and then hanging or laying them flat to dry. A few garments can be fluffed in the dryer on a low setting. I take these instructions very seriously, and the time investment has paid off. I kid you not—I have owned and worn certain classic designer pieces for years, and they look brand-new because I take *special* care of them.

I want you to think of yourself as the most beautifully designed pair of slacks walking a New York runway. I'm thinking Stella McCartney's Chellini trousers. Yes, you're pricey—$1,375 last time I checked. You hang perfectly—no bunching, no binding, and—oh—check out that rear! You are the perfect size and length, making legs look long and lean. You're the most gorgeous, intense color ever found, and your fabric is divine; you are soft and comfortable and you never wrinkle.

But imagine that instead of being washed on the gentle cycle in cool water, you get thrown in a tub of hot water with an orange hoodie on a cycle spinning at 1,800 RPMs. Instead of being hung gently to drip-dry, you are placed in the dryer with a pair of sneakers and a few pairs of Levi's 501 jeans. Do you come out looking refreshed and renewed? Of course not! You come out of the wash looking completely worn out! This is no way to be treated; you deserve better than this.

You are the most beautifully made and priceless person in the world to your family, and you must be given special care. So over the next eighteen days, I'm taking over your laundry. Ha! Not really. But I do hope to encourage you to remember that you are important and that to last a lifetime, you must take special care of yourself as you consciously consider those things that will refresh your mind and body in order to renew your spirit.

> I know the LORD is always with me. I will not be shaken, for he is right beside me. . . . You will show me the way of life, granting me the joy of your presence and the pleasures of living with you forever. **PSALM 16:8, 11**

I can't believe how much I enjoy writing about laundry. If this devotional thing doesn't work out, I think I'll try my hand at a jingle for Tide.

WHAT YOU LEFT
AT THE HOSPITAL

SHAUNA AND ADAM WERE completely incredulous the day they brought our granddaughter, Ava, their seven-day-old preemie, home from the hospital. As Steve and I helped them to the car, Adam looked at me, eyes wide, and said, "I can't believe they just let us walk out of there with her." Yep. No manual. No contract. No warranty. Just a real live human being swaddled in a fuzzy pink blanket. Good luck!

Driving home with a brand-spanking-new kid is relatively simple. But keeping any new mom's identity intact while she learns to be Mommy to one, or now to two or more, is something else.

In Kathryn Stockett's book *The Help*, protagonist Aibileen is a wise domestic who understands that her most important role is shaping the mind, heart, and soul of the child she has charge over. Aibileen knows that what we are taught to believe about ourselves is what we become. As she holds the little blonde girl on her lap, she recites the most important nine words in the saga:

"You is kind. You is smart. You is important."[1]

I would like to recite those nine words to you because somewhere between the epidural and the healing of your episiotomy, I suspect you may have forgotten this.

You don't just *act* nice—you have an incredible heart. You are thoughtful, you are generous, you are kind to your core. Your light shines brightly on those around you.

You're not just lucky at what you pull off—you are amazing! Your mind is open, your intellect grows each day, you hold the equivalent of a doctorate in family management. And you may be doing it while juggling a forty-plus-hour-a-week job outside the home!

You're not "just" Mom—you are the glue of your family. You idealize, you develop, and you manage the future influencers and leaders of our country. Mom, no one I know has the power to impact change for our world as much as you.

You may rarely hear these words because your kids (if they're over the age of nine) might think you're as dumb as a doorknob, your husband is *still* distracted with his own post-delivery issues, and those of us who benefit from your kindness, intellect, and leadership forget it is you who hold the keys to our future civilization.

As he thinks in his heart, so is he.　**PROVERBS 23:7**, NKJV

"You is kind. You is smart. You is important." Now, just ponder *that* as you sit in the car-pool line.

SOMETHING'S GONNA BLOW

IF YOU DIDN'T GET THE CHANCE to build an erupting volcano when you were in grade school, never fear, your kids will probably get the assignment. That will give you the opportunity either to create one again or to enjoy a virgin voyage into the world of volcano making. Either way, you'll be up all hours of the night building the base, dripping in papier-mâché, and testing the explosive recipe. When everything comes together, it's a blast—unlike some of our *personal* eruptions.

How and why do the children of our wombs elicit such exasperation? Because we're a walking, talking science-fair volcano recipe ready to blow at any minute:

We're emotionally invested = ½ c. water
We're physically drained = ¼ c. vinegar
We're overscheduled = ¼ c. dish detergent
We're spiritually bankrupt = red food coloring
And they're sinners = THE BAKING SODA

This is not a good combination.

To neutralize our recipe for disaster, let's look at what we could take out of the mix. Since we carried these human beings *inside our bodies* or perhaps stayed up nights pacing, awaiting word that our baby had been born, it's likely we'll stay emotionally invested in them until the day we die. My kids are in their thirties, and I am as deeply invested in their welfare today as I was when I found out that I was pregnant with the first one and that my second one was awaiting my adoption.

This leaves us with the next three things in our concoction for explosion: physical exhaustion, a crammed schedule, and spiritual bankruptcy. Each of these is within our control. When was your last Sabbath? Stop laughing. I'm serious. When did you last take time to rest? You might not get a full day to yourself until your kids leave for college, but that doesn't mean you can't take at least sixty minutes once a week right now. You *have* to fit rest into your life. And when you take that time, do something you love or luxuriate in doing nothing at all. Embrace it mentally and emotionally as *your* Sabbath for refreshment.

Identifying what comes between your being a good mom and your being a great mom requires reflection and discipline. Say no to those things that encroach on your brain cells. Being overscheduled is more of a mental stressor than a physical one. Show me a mom with a quiet mind, and I'll show you a mom with self-control.

Everyone experiences spiritual bankruptcy, whether they have kids or not. It comes from neglecting time for prayer, the study of God's Word, and worship. Like the red food coloring in the volcano mix, spiritual insolvency stains everything. Your investment in your spiritual bank account is totally within your control. So when might you make such a deposit? On your Sabbath!

This leaves us with our precious little sinners. The ones who take Magic Markers to the freshly painted walls (Scott, age three) and the ones who sneak a wine cooler from the garage fridge (Shauna, age fifteen). Sometimes they will make questionable, even very bad, decisions. Our kids will always be our baking soda.

> The creation of the heavens and the earth and everything in them was completed. On the seventh day God had finished his work of creation, so he rested from all his work. **GENESIS 2:1-2**

Sweet sister, we have to get control of the family schedule by saying no. We must invest in our spiritual bank account. And we need some time off. That investment will lessen our physical, mental, and spiritual exhaustion, leaving us with "only" our emotional investment (water) and a precious little sinner (baking soda). When those two mix, we might get a little fizz, but nothing that will blow.

FIND TIME TO SOAK;
TAKE TIME TO PRAY

WHEN WAS THE LAST TIME you lit a candle, ran a hot tub of bubbles, and became so relaxed you needed a pair of water wings to keep you afloat? Can't remember? Then you're either the mother of a toddler or the mom of kids in soccer, dance, piano, and tae kwon do. *A bath?* Ha! I bet you go days without even washing your hair!

Alone time is a *luxury* most moms rarely get to enjoy. Once the kids are past the clingy stage, you're in high demand for carpooling, helping with homework, and cheer-leading from the stands. Some moms balance all this while juggling conference calls, pacifying demanding clients, and writing *War and Peace*–length e-mails to their bosses after the kids are in bed.

And this is how some good Christian moms find themselves in an extramarital affair.

A couple of years ago I became a fan of the TV series *Parenthood*. I really enjoyed the program; the writers did a great job of capturing the best and worst of families. In the next-to-last season, one of the women, Julia, lost her job as an attorney and was thrust into a stay-at-home mom role for which she wasn't well suited. You might say her "lather-rinse-repeat" lifestyle grew monotonous; the day-in-day-out rou-tine of her grade-schoolers was not a world she had imagined inhabiting 24-7. While volunteering at her kids' school, Julia struck up a friendship with a stay-at-home dad. And the friendship blossomed.

I wanted to scream at Julia: "*Guard your heart!*"

Sweet, witty, smart, pretty Julia didn't set out to have an affair. She was an incredibly devoted mom and wife (unfortunately, her hunk of a husband had become distracted by work). Julia's friendship with the classmate's dad started innocently as they volunteered together on a project. But Julia found herself thinking more and more about this guy and how he made her feel. Julia didn't have a chance because she didn't see *it* coming.

Moms, we might not have an affair, but we can be led astray. That's why we have to find a few minutes alone each day with God. Time spent in prayer is not a luxury but a vital necessity for protecting our marriage, children, reputation, and walk with Christ.

We pour every ounce we have into those kids in the next room. We fuss over the house; we worry over work; we manage our household budget like the CFO of a publicly traded company. But when we fail to invest in our own minds, hearts, and souls, we give the enemy a foothold from which to completely unravel our lives.

Guard your heart above all else, for it determines the course of your life.   **PROVERBS 4:23**

Sister, carve out some quiet time to study God's Word. Guard your heart. And pray like your life depends on it. Because it does.

COMING TO THE RESCUE

HONEY, WHAT ARE YOU THINKING? Oh, sorry, Mom. Not you. This entry is for your husband. You might want to pass the book over to him for just a sec.

Darlin', while you're out saving the world (and making a buck), your damsel is in distress. God certainly made men and women different (and for that I say hallelujah!), but I'm worried that some of you Supermen don't see that your Lois Lane is in trouble.

Tell me: Is she irritable? Let me ask you straight up—does she nag? Is she emotional—do you never know what mood she's going to be in on any given night? Is she "unavailable" after 10:00 p.m.—can't remember the last time she came on to you? Do you feel invisible—does she seem not even to know you live in the same house?

Well, Clark, here's the problem: She's overwhelmed. And even with your X-ray vision, you likely don't see it. After all, you may work hard at a demanding job to provide for your family and then spend your weekends keeping the yard ship-shape. You may even coach your kids' sports team. But your Lois is at her wit's end.

For various reasons, husbands don't always understand how much their wives are stretched by their multiple roles: lover, mother, housekeeper, chef, tutor, cheerleader, and taxi driver. And even if you recognize the problem, you might be perplexed by how to help. But you know what? She's looking for you—her husband, *her protector*, to come to her rescue. She's drowning in a sea of 24-7 obligations, and you may not even be throwing her an inflatable swim ring!

I know you love her. And I know you really do want to help, so I'm going to tell you what you can do to save the day.

Wake up. Help set the tone of the day for everyone, bright and early. Make breakfast. Pack lunches. Fill bottles. Make beds. Drive the kids to school. Just volunteer to do a few things to lighten her load as the day gets started. But do it every day, and do it like she would do it—with finesse, joy, and love.

Get up. Her day doesn't end at 6:00 p.m. She may even be coming home from a job that's as demanding as yours. But now her second job begins. So put in a load of laundry. Help with homework. Cook dinner. Take bath duty. Referee the fight between your two daughters before they tear each other's hair out. Just come to her rescue in the evenings, lifting the weight of household duties off her shoulders, and do so with finesse, love, and joy.

Suck it up. Motherhood is the most sacrificial role on the face of the planet. She will give up anything and everything for the care and well-being of you and those kids. Well, you can do that too. Walk the baby with colic. Clean up the vomit. Pass on the Saturday golf game. Take dance recital *dress rehearsal* duty. (Ugh. Now she'll know you've *really* come in for the rescue!)

> In the same way, husbands ought to love their wives as they love their own bodies. For a man who loves his wife actually shows love for himself. **EPHESIANS 5:28**

Superman, your sweet wife cannot be responsible for everything and everyone, every minute of every day. It's time to step up. When you do, you just might be surprised at how much more time she has for you.

WHAT YOU WORRY ABOUT THAT YOU SHOULDN'T

LET'S START TODAY'S DEVOTION with this question: What do you *not* worry about? It's a mother's job to worry. Right?

We worry about paying the bills: Regardless of how much money we make, there's always another expense looming.

We worry about our kids' academic development: Reading is not coming easy to him.

We worry about our marriage: We never talk about anything but the kids.

We worry about our jobs: They are so demanding and yet we never feel totally secure.

We worry about saving: That college scholarship may not come through.

We worry about our teen's date tonight: Actually, maybe we *do* need to worry about this one, but you get my point.

Net-net, we worry about everything—especially what we cannot possibly control. As moms we're often in charge of planning and executing, so we feel we must strategize, and to strategize *we must think of all the things that could go wrong.* When we *think of all the things that could go wrong,* we become fearful.

Excessive fear is kindling for the bonfire of anguish. Our overactive imaginations conjure up all kinds of disasters for our families, completely derailing our sense of peace and our exercise of faith. The way I see it, there are two major contributors to our fear:

1. We haven't prayed. And I mean *really* prayed—not the "Hey, God, help the kids today at school" type of prayers as we drop them off. Oh, those are important prayers, but if we want to stop worrying, we have to sit down, eliminate all distractions, and pour out our hearts. We must get specific as to what we're praying for. Let's write our prayers down. Say them out loud. Make it a real conversation. We have to pray specifically over our fear if we want to eliminate worry.

2. Often when we do pray, we don't believe we'll get the answer we want. *How in the world can God fix this? Does God even really care about this issue?* Or the grandpappy of them all: *Maybe God's answer is no—now I really need to worry! How can God's will and his divine plan be better than what I want?*

Coming from me, the woman whose kid was strung out on meth and missing for three and a half years, I know these prayer challenges like the back of my hand. I was once the mom who worried about *everything* and tried to manage my fears myself, until I had a big, big *something* right in front of me. I can tell you that I didn't get it until I was faced with a crisis so deadly, I had no other option than to believe and to turn all my fears over to the Lord. Without faith in our God, that he's got this—whatever "this" is—we'll never have peace. Oswald Chambers said it succinctly: "The remarkable thing about God is that when you fear God, you fear nothing else, whereas if you do not fear God, you fear everything else."[2]

Don't worry about anything; instead, pray about everything.
Tell God what you need, and thank him for all he has done.
PHILIPPIANS 4:6

To put worry at bay, pray specifically and *give* your every fear to God. Then grab yourself a cup of coffee and say a prayer of praise for the mighty work he will do, according to his will and his perfect timetable. For you see, he *already has* this. Feel better?

MOM MESSED UP

Sometimes we lose our cool; if you're like me, nothing makes you feel worse than when you lose it with your kids. Even moms with the self-control of a Benedictine monk will sometimes mess up.

Self-control was not one of my mom's top ten strengths. She had many redeeming qualities, but she suffered from bipolar disorder, so self-regulation was not a "gift of the Spirit" that she carried in her fruit basket (see Galatians 5:22-23).

The season was summer, the day a Sunday; I was twelve at the time. I loved to swim, but the municipal pool was an eleven-mile drive to the city. My parents and I had talked earlier in the week about them dropping me off at the pool that Sunday. So when I asked if we were going to go, I was completely stunned at my mom's response.

She lost it. Bad. With a belt.

It was the first time I had ever been really afraid. Within seconds I moved from being frightened of childish things like ghosts and the wind to being adult-afraid for my safety. It was a pivotal day in our relationship—not because she beat me, but because she never apologized.

By that age I had learned to expect the unexpected. Those who live with an addict or someone who suffers from mental illness know this is just the way you roll. So the beating over a trivial offense (I just asked if we were going to the pool) humiliated me, but it was not what created the gaping wound that would ooze for years to come.

When Mom settled down, I knew that she knew she was wrong. What I couldn't wrap my little chlorine-bleached head around was why she didn't admit her mistake and apologize to me. Instead, she brought the ordeal up again, days, weeks, and even many years later, insisting that I had caused her overreaction.

Humility is an attribute critical to establishing and strengthening relationships, and nowhere should your humility be more evident than when you mess up with your kids. Even when your kids are grown, you might find (as I have) that your tone can bite and your words can sting. The soothing salve of "Please forgive me. I was wrong to react that way" helps heal those wounds that can otherwise fester over time.

The faithful love of the LORD never ends! His mercies never cease. Great is his faithfulness; his mercies begin afresh each morning. **LAMENTATIONS 3:22-23**

Mom, try to keep your cool. But when you do lose it, remember that every mom messes up. Just say you're sorry and mean it so you can both start fresh tomorrow.

UNDER THE INFLUENCE

IF YOUR KIDS ARE STILL YOUNG, I warn you now—after spending a lifetime with you, they're going to know immediately when something's up. And if they love you, they're going to call you out.

"Mom, what's going on with you?"

As my nearly thirty-year-old daughter sat in front of me, she respectfully poured out her concern. She noticed I was being affected by some new acquaintances and, clearly, not for the better. It seems my preoccupation with fashion trends and my personal appearance, along with an onslaught of new social engagements, was becoming unbecoming. Whoa. This was some serious role reversal. During her impromptu one-on-one "intervention," she provided me a few specific examples, then sweetly affirmed that she loved me. (Of course I knew she wanted to say, "But you're making me nuts.")

I wish I could tell you this exchange happened many years ago, but in reality it occurred as I was turning fifty. Yes. Five-oh. How in the world had I fallen under the influence of others at the midpoint of my life? How was this even possible?

Upon reflection, I realized that we are all impacted by the people we engage with, regardless of our age. In addition, social media and our fascination with celebrities can also, when allowed to, augment or detract from our true selves. Like Shauna, I have watched people I care for "lose themselves" to the well-meaning counsel of others or the pull of social trends. What made these women unique, interesting, and endearing was watered down and sometimes washed out by another's influence. Nick Pitts, in his *Daily Briefing*, April 19, 2016, said it really well: "It is increasingly necessary to remind ourselves that we are not who we think we are, or who others say we are, or what we feel we are, but we are who God says we are: beloved (Romans 1:7)."

Perhaps you've been influenced by women in your Bible study to deepen your relationship with Christ. Or maybe someone at work has made a mark on your professional development. Not all influencers are bad. But some can be. And this is why we need to stop and take a inventory.

Who is influencing you, today? Are they daughters of the King? What positive attributes do they bring to your life, your family, and your walk with Christ? Or have lemmings snuck into your social circle, convincing you to invest precious brain cells in things that don't matter one iota? You'll know it if the influence looks superficial or if the changes in your behavior, values, or appearance are not really "you." Whom you hang out with matters as much as whom your kids hang out with. Be careful of your peer group.

We will no longer be immature like children. We won't be tossed and blown about by every wind of new teaching. We will not be influenced when people try to trick us with lies so clever they sound like the truth. **EPHESIANS 4:14**

Ask yourself if you're seeking the approval of others or of God. Realize that you could be pulled offtrack at any age, and notice it yourself—before your kids point it out. Trust me. It's really embarrassing when you're on the other side of a "talking-to."

CHECK YOUR GURU'S CREDENTIALS

IF YESTERDAY'S READING has you thinking that perhaps you'd benefit from some good, godly counsel, let me advise you to check your counselor's credentials carefully. My daughter, Shauna, always seems to be the one who provides me "truth in love." This time in a dressing room, circa 1995.

Shopping for an upcoming vacation, we hit the swimsuit department. Loaded with suits in an array of styles and colors, we located dressing rooms across the aisle from each other. We'd change into a suit, giggle, and say "*Ready!*" as we simultaneously opened our doors.

With every style she tried on, I'd tell my eighteen-year-old daughter (sporting a Barbie doll figure) how adorable she looked. (Unless she looked *too* adorable, in which case we'd opt for one with more fabric.) With every style I tried on, she'd study me with a knitted brow. "Hmm . . . try the blue one." And then, "Try the green one." Or "Try . . ." You get the picture.

Finally I asked, "What? None of these look cute?" With a sheepish smile, she pointed to my breasts and said, "Mom, have you ever thought about making those bigger?"

Give me a break.

My fashion guru is correct in that I am not a full-figured woman. I still have the build of a fourteen-year-old boy. But . . . I did not *need augmentation*! No. I just needed more padding!

My guru and I were looking at the world from very different perspectives. She was focused on my chest, outward; I was focused on my chest, inward. I know I only have a limited number of brain cells available and can use them to the benefit of vanity, obsessing over calories, Botox injections, boob jobs, clothes, hairstyles, makeup, and every morsel I put in my mouth—or I can use them to obsess over service, God's Word, the condition of my soul, how I make others feel, and every "Kingdom" thought I allow in my head. I can focus on my chest outward, or my chest inward. Doing both is tricky.

So here's the lesson: Seek an influencer who walks with Christ, not the world. Seek an influencer who has succeeded in building a successful life in spite of difficulty or recurring setbacks. Seek an influencer whose faith you admire. Seek an influencer who is discerning: one who is tactful and cares for you enough to speak the truth. Discern through prayer if that counsel is godly and whether you'd be following God's will or someone else's should you heed that advice. When you're operating under the influence, make sure it is his.

As iron sharpens iron, so a friend sharpens a friend.
PROVERBS 27:17

And never go shopping for a swimsuit with an eighteen-year-old.

LONGING FOR CHILD'S POSE

MY LEGS WERE SHAKING UNCONTROLLABLY. My arms felt like fifty-pound weights. Every muscle in my body screamed as sweat poured from my hairline, stinging my eyes. I was completely spent. And this is what I chose to do for fun this morning.

What was different about my 6:00 a.m. yoga class today? I pushed myself beyond what I was physically capable of doing.

I was exhausted. And I'll bet you a dollar to a doughnut you are too. But probably not due to anything you did at the gym.

Exhaustion (not just hormones) is our enemy, transforming us from sweet, confident women to raving lunatics. It affects every relationship we have, and probably none more than our relationship with Christ. Exhaustion comes in a wide variety of packages—physical, mental, emotional, and spiritual—but each has a similar cause:

A failure to recognize our physical limitations (*Of course I can wrap my leg around my head!*)

Reluctance to admit our frailty (*Me? Frail? I am as strong as an ox.*)

Impatience with the process (*I've been at this for four months. Good grief! I should be a yogi by now!*)

A competitive spirit (*If you can stand on one leg with the other extended vertically over your head, I'm absolutely sure I can do it too.*)

A willingness to sacrifice self-care (*No pain; no gain. I'm going to do this if it kills me.*)

The inability to discern the important from the critical (*I believe it's more important for me to twist myself like a pretzel today than be able to walk tomorrow.*)

A lack of confidence to delegate (*I wouldn't give you my yoga mat and 6:00 a.m. reservation if I could; I'm sure you wouldn't do it the way I wanted you to.*)

The bottom line is, our pride is often at the root of our exhaustion. We think we *must*. When really, for the sake of our sanity and those we love, we *must not*.

If you find yourself longing for child's pose—or worse, curled up in the fetal position—let me remind you: Exhaustion may be normal by the world's standard, but it is not biblical. God cannot use us when we're spent. He needs us at our peak. And to be at our best, we must sleep, we must eat well, we must breathe deeply, and we must laugh heartily. He needs us alert, nourished, clearheaded, and joyful so that when he calls us to serve him or our family, we can do it well.

> Those who trust in the LORD will find new strength. They will soar high on wings like eagles. They will run and not grow weary. They will walk and not faint. **ISAIAH 40:31**

Don't let your pride (or those kids) wear you out. Now, let's all take a big, deep breath. Hold it. And, together, let it out. Ahhh.

LET IT GO

No, I'm not going to share the lyrics to the *Frozen* theme song—we've all heard plenty of that one. But I do want to visit with you about letting go of grief—specifically the sadness and mourning that can accompany our sin or the wrongs committed against us.

Good girls, *God's girls*, sometimes make very bad decisions. We lose ourselves, only to wake up in a sweat from the nightmare that started as a dream (sin has a way of looking alluring at first). As if the sin weren't bad enough, now our relationships and maybe even our lives are derailed by our oppression and grief. Sister, grief will gut the life out of you—and everyone you love.

I don't know what you've done. Those you've sinned against may not even know. It doesn't matter. You know, and the sadness over what you've done is killing you. That remorse is unwinding the promise of a life lived to its fullest with joy.

Somehow, it's often easier for us to accept forgiveness from God than to extend it to ourselves. But if we don't intellectually and emotionally cover our own sweet, sinful heads with grace, the fallout of our sin continues to haunt us.

There is also a grief that results from being sinned against. A deep hurt. A relationship ended. Hopes, dreams, sometimes even innocence, lost forever. This grief often groans deep within.

My mom had a lot of challenges, and as I think back on the aftermath of some of her mistakes, I remember as a little girl watching her grieve. I knew she was mourning not only her own mistakes but also the wrongs done to her. Her grief compounded her depression. Her depression made an already tense household more stressful. And the stress we each bore from her inability to let it go spread throughout our family like a cancer.

Because time can't be turned back to right a wrong, grief often settles in. This is not an emotion we should ignore or attempt to deal with alone. Professional counsel, lay counselors such as Stephen Ministers, books on grief, and long talks with a friend are wonderful resources as you learn to give the loss to Christ.

Mom was a Christian; she knew Christ forgave her and others. She just couldn't forgive herself. Grief ultimately did her in—and on some days, it did us in, too.

> I am dying from grief; my years are shortened by sadness. Sin has drained my strength; I am wasting away from within. **PSALM 31:10**

Sweet friend, don't let your sin (or those of others) further derail your world or that of your family. Life is too short, and your family is too precious. Let it go.

CHEAPER THAN THERAPY

MOMS ARE THE MOST SACRIFICIAL LAMBS walking the face of the earth. There is nothing we won't give up for our kids.

We will go without new clothes or a professional style and color to see that our children have what they need (and want).

We will eat lunch on the run as we taxi kids to activities, or down breakfast behind the wheel as we dash off to work. We give up Zumba class and live on a diet void of all major food groups (with the exception of lattes—there's milk in them). Anything longer than a five-hour stretch of zzzz's at one time is considered sleeping in.

We forfeit dinner with our friends, lunch and shopping with our own moms, and Saturday afternoon dates with our husbands. If our friends and family aren't in the mommy playgroup, serving at the school, or sitting on the bleachers, we lose track of them. All the important people who bring richness to our lives mysteriously fade away.

Then one day, our sweet little cherubs morph into hormonal zombies who either don't recognize or don't appreciate the sacrifices we've made over the previous fourteen years. Their attitude is one of entitlement, which leaves us seething as we count to ten when we really want to slap them silly.

I'm just saying. This is what happens. Not always, of course. But mostly.

Here's the takeaway for you: Be careful for whom and what you're willing to sacrifice. It could backfire years later in the form of poor health, crushing disappointment, lost opportunity, loneliness, and sometimes even depression.

We give of ourselves until we're empty. We abandon relationships only to awaken after the kids are gone and realize that there's no one in our circle because there are no games or school carnivals to attend.

Go get your hair done. Sit down at the table to eat. Take a break from the games this Saturday to spend a two-hour lunch with your mom, your sister, or a friend.

> He lets me rest in green meadows; he leads me beside peaceful streams. He renews my strength. **PSALM 23:2-3**

Then, when pubescent Johnny spouts off with a statement that starts with "You never . . . ," you won't be tempted to knock him into tomorrow. You won't need medication or a therapist either because you will not have needlessly sacrificed your own long-term well-being for the sake of your child's temporal entertainment. Trust me. It's temporary.

UNTAPPED POTENTIAL

WHEN YOU SEE YOUR KIDS UNDERACHIEVING, doesn't it make your stomach turn? You see their capacity to problem solve, their ability to memorize, their athletic prowess, their artistic bent, and their performance abilities. And then you watch them squander it, whine, take it for granted, and fail to embrace the deep reservoir of their potential.

Imagine now that you're God. Watching us. Oh my.

I have no doubt that you and I have been designed for greatness. At every age and at every life stage, God has something important for us to do.

Gladys Burrill and Harriette Thompson were not trained runners when they ran their first marathons at ages eighty-six and seventy-six, respectively. These gals have completed several marathons since and are recorded as the oldest female marathon runners: Gladys at the age of ninety-two years and nineteen days and Harriette at ninety-two years and sixty-five days old.[3] If they can cover more than twenty-six miles in one stretch, surely I can master standing on my head before I turn sixty.

Julia Child, whose career had been in advertising, was never seriously interested in cooking until she enrolled at Le Cordon Bleu cooking school in Paris at the age of thirty-seven. After cowriting her famous cookbook, she hosted her first TV cooking show, *The French Chef*, at fifty. At first glance—and oh, at the first sound of that voice!—she was an unlikely character for broadcast. But the gal created an entire industry and is a legend to those of us who love to cook.

After her first book was rejected by publishers, Laura Ingalls Wilder, a former teacher, mother, and farmer's wife, kept at it and reworked her manuscript until it was picked up. *Little House in the Big Woods*, the first in her beloved children's series, was published when Laura was sixty-five; her last book hit the shelves as she turned seventy-six. What discipline, tenacity, and confidence.

These women all felt an urging; each was strong and courageous, bold and daring. God calls us throughout our lives to embrace our "what's next" with enthusiasm, determination, and wide-eyed wonder as we consider what he might have in store for *us*. Like these fabulous women, our job is to answer the call.

> I also pray that you will understand the incredible greatness of God's power for us who believe him. This is the same mighty power that raised Christ from the dead and seated him in the place of honor at God's right hand in the heavenly realms. **EPHESIANS 1:19-20**

So don't give me this crapola that you're too old, your résumé is dated, or your experience is irrelevant. You, my friend, are destined for greatness for his glory. Be prepared for what is to come.

A TRAGIC DEATH

The Story Teller's Book, circa 1912, includes this riveting tale:

> One day as Chicken Licken was scratching under the pea vines in the barnyard a pea fell out of a pod and struck her on the head.
>
> "Oh!" said Chicken Licken, "the sky is falling! I must go and tell the king."[4]

(Never mind that she jumped to a ridiculous conclusion without all the facts—that's a lesson we can cover another time.) Back to the story: Chicken Licken headed off to find the king and along the way ran into her friend, Henny Penny; but she didn't really give Henny Penny the facts as they actually happened. Chicken Licken reported that she saw the sky falling and heard it with her own ears as the sky fell on her tail. Henny Penny was convinced by the dramatization of the story and went with her to find the king. Along the way they told the same story to other friends, picking up support from Cocky Locky, Ducky Lucky, and Turkey Lurkey.

As they went deeper into the woods, Foxy Loxy greeted the crazed-out birds, and they shared the "news" with him with great excitement. He volunteered to take them to the king (since they hadn't a clue where to find him) but, of course, escorted them to his den instead. There they died at the hands of Foxy Loxy. The details given are not graphic, but they are tragic.

This poignant tale illustrates how unfounded rumors and gossip spread with devastating effect. It also says something about our inclination toward negativity and our flare for the dramatic, neither of which we will find listed among the fruits of the Spirit.

Whether we're the subject of a rumor or we're part of the crew generating the drama, gossip poisons us all. Gossip kills joy—we can't talk negatively about others and feel joyful when we're finished. Gossip destroys love—we certainly don't feel loved when we're being slandered. Gossip obliterates peace—there's no peace when we find out our friends are talking behind our backs, nor is there peace in the middle of the night for those of us who spread falsehoods, only to be awakened by the Holy Spirit. Kindness and goodness? Poisoned for those participating and the sweet soul whose heart has been broken.

How about this for a remedy? What if we all vowed never again to engage in gossip? If we did, gossip in our social circles would end. And the fruit of the Spirit would spill *abundantly* all around us and through us.

> Their lives became full of every kind of wickedness, sin, greed, hate, envy, murder, quarreling, deception, malicious behavior, and gossip. **ROMANS 1:29**

Gossip—listed right there with murder and wickedness. It kills joy from the inside out.

THE PITIFUL ELM

NOTHING DRAINS A PERSON'S spirit faster than feeling unappreciated or, worse, discounted. Once this terrible realization begins to creep in—when we suspect that others may be disparaging us—our joy is consumed by self-doubt and insecurity, which creates a downward spiral in our attitude and productivity. Over weeks and months, the rejection we suspected becomes expected. If you can relate, allow me to share with you the story of our pitiful elm tree.

When Steve and I built our home, we had to remove a couple of significantly sized trees. Because we love nature (and because it was a city requirement), we replaced the trees with majestic beauties, which would be transplanted as soon as the construction was complete. However, before they arrived, a city inspector stopped by and was adamant that one be planted now—like, that day—to get our building inspection approved. It didn't matter that we had ordered and were installing massive trees the next week. He wanted one planted pronto. Okay. Fine.

One of our contractors ran off to fetch us a tree, and what he returned with was the saddest-looking little elm you've ever seen. The poor thing looked completely out of place and out of proportion to the house, but it did its job. It got us a green tag, so we were good to go with the remainder of our construction. Knowing we had a gorgeous tree for that particular spot on its way, Steve and I decided that we'd just take the elm out and give it to the contractor when the trees we ordered came in.

Days later, when the transplanting of the large trees began in earnest, we decided to move the pitiful elm temporarily to the edge of our courtyard. However, when we looked out from the living room the next morning, we couldn't believe it—it was as if that tree was made for that spot. A year later, it is beautiful, growing mightily, and will likely be one of our most important trees for shading and fall color!

We had unwittingly discounted the tree, when in reality it was just what we needed. There was nothing wrong with the tree; there was something wrong with the way we looked at it and what we expected from it.

Sister, if you're in a tough place right now—not feeling like you quite fit or belong in a certain situation—and your confidence is waning, hear this: You are not a throwaway tree. Chances are you have been created for something different from what is expected of you, or perhaps you just need to be moved. You might need room to expand your branches in order to throw your shade on a different side of the office or on a new committee. But you are and will continue to be a person of great value. Feelings of failure or a lack of confidence can drain your spirit, causing you to feel pitiful when, in fact, you are glorious!

> Thank you for making me so wonderfully complex! Your workmanship is marvelous—how well I know it. **PSALM 139:14**

Know your worth. Love those who discount you. I know—it's hard, but don't believe them for a minute. You were wonderfully *made* to do something wonderful.

WORKIN' NINE TO FIVE

DON'T YOU WISH YOUR WORKING HOURS were only nine to five? An eight-hour workday is the most hilarious concept a mother has ever heard of. All moms work nearly a twenty-four-hour day. During a single rotation of the earth around the sun, some moms also go to an office or other workplace and toil at their second job.

Much has been written and discussed about the Mommy Wars for nearly thirty years. It's an interesting phenomenon that pits out-of-home working moms against stay-at-home working moms. But it's really not a war. It's judgment. And that's a fight no one wins.

It baffles me that this argument continues to rage today: working moms who defend and justify their decision to work outside the home (note: lots of moms don't *get to choose*; if the bills are to be paid, they work) against working moms who defend and justify their decision to stay at home. It makes me want to whisper-scream: *You're completely missing God's point.*

Some of the godliest women I know are absolutely pre-disposed to have a career. One of my best friends, Kathryn, is a doctor. She was not looking to escape caring for her three children. God had hardwired her to be a doctor, and she is also a fabulous mother and grandmother.

On the other hand, some of the godliest women I know are absolutely designed to stay home. Another one of my

34

best friends, Stacie, a mom with four kids under the age of fourteen, left her very successful career when she had her first baby. It is not that she wanted to escape the workplace; God had just designed her to invest most of her mental and physical energy into the development of her kids. She, like Kathryn, is a fabulous mother.

Don't be a Judge Judy. Instead, respect your sisters in Christ. Remember who they are in God's sight. Build them up with words of encouragement, and pray that God would supply them with the mental and physical energy they need as they go about their days, handling stressful workloads. God has given us each gifts, desires, and talents according to his purpose.

> He makes the whole body fit together perfectly. As each part does its own special work, it helps the other parts grow, so that the whole body is healthy and growing and full of love. **EPHESIANS 4:16**

Most important, dear friend, don't judge yourself. Embrace the mom and woman whom God made you to be. Together, as the body of Christ, we'll get these kiddos raised.

PRAY THIS, NOT THAT

I LOVE THE POPULAR BOOK SERIES Eat This, Not That! by David Zinczenko and Matt Goulding. Any book that leads with pictures of ice cream and hamburgers (two of my favorites) on a book cover and encourages me to eat up is a bestseller on my list!

These books offer insight and information on the fat, sodium, and calories that are hidden in many of the foods we eat. So often (and this is the part I love), they inform us that salads are a far less healthy choice than pasta! Again—how can you not love these books?

Sometimes even less obvious than what we should eat is what we should pray. I'm afraid there are times when I have prayed for only what I've wanted and not for the outcome that will glorify God. My prayers can sometimes be self-centered and small.

In *Mere Christianity*, C. S. Lewis wrote, "He is building quite a different house from the one you thought of—throwing out a new wing here, putting on an extra floor there, running up towers, making courtyards. You thought you were going to be made into a decent little cottage: but He is building a palace. He intends to come and live in it Himself."[6] Our prayers should be for our good—but more important for his glory.

And this is why I pray for flavor and favor, not razzle and dazzle.

In my position as president of a marketing agency, I frequently stand before an audience. Whether speaking to frustrated employees, anxious clients, or an audience of my peers, I must be very careful with my words. My remarks must be clear. My tone, inviting. My motives, pure. My words, inspiring. In a nutshell, my number one job is to instill confidence.

This has led me to a new place of prayer. Rather than ask for the blessing of clarity of mind and voice or for a stage presence that will leave the gathering in awe of my cleverness, I find myself immensely blessed when I humbly ask for flavor and favor. Flavor, that my words, tone, inflection, and body language will be seasoned by his grace and will bless my listeners. And favor, that my audience will hear me with their hearts first and their minds second. That they will know my motives are pure and my intent is for their success, not just my own.

> Let your conversation be always full of grace, seasoned with salt, so that you may know how to answer everyone.
> **COLOSSIANS 4:6, NIV**

As you address your peers or employees at work, the PTA, your home owners' association, or your women's group, trade the petition of razzle-dazzle for flavor-favor. Your impact will extend far beyond Thursday night's meeting. You're going to be great! *For him.*

day 18

IF YOU ONLY REMEMBER THIS

WHEN I READ A BOOK, I often get to the end and wonder, *So what was the point of all that?* As we close out this first section that's all about your well-being, I would like to leave you with one concept. If you don't remember another word I wrote, remember this: Fortify yourself.

I pray you will press this imperative on your heart and allow it to permeate your mind because I believe it will carry you through the best and worst of days ahead. Days when you're on your last nerve. Days when you're confused. Days when you've scaled that mountain of motherhood and are at your very best.

To fortify yourself means that you purposefully strengthen your body, mind, and soul against attack: physical, emotional, and spiritual. When you are well fortified, you are prepared to play defense and resist forces that are greater than you.

When you fortify yourself, you take action to build your endurance. You are vigorous, full of energy, and prepared for those days when your high-octane kids most need you to be at the top of your game.

When you fortify yourself, you greatly increase your effectiveness—like taking vitamins. You are nourished. Good stuff is happening inside you that you can't see or even feel. But trust me, everyone will know if you're deficient.

When you fortify yourself, you strengthen your resolve. You can do nothing without Christ. And he can't do much with you if you're not committed to him.

The LORD will guide you continually, giving you water
when you are dry and restoring your strength. You will
be like a well-watered garden, like an ever-flowing spring.
ISAIAH 58:11

When you're nourished, you flourish. Fortify yourself.
We're all depending on you.

I SAID THIS PRAYER *for You* LAST NIGHT

YOU MIGHT THINK IT STRANGE that I prayed for you last night.
But I did.

God has placed you on my heart. Although I don't know you,
I feel as if you've been my friend forever. And because I care so
deeply for you, I want you to know that this is what I prayed:

---

*Our heavenly Father, I pray you will bless my friend with eyes
to see herself as you see her—as your glorious daughter destined
for greatness on this earth and for your Kingdom. I pray that
you will send the Holy Spirit to be a constant reminder of her
critical impact on our society through her role as a mom, and I
ask you to empower her with the good sense to carve out a time
of Sabbath for her rest and the discipline to take it.*

*I ask that you will shower her with opportunities as she
prepares for greatness and the fulfillment of her untapped
potential. Bless her with discernment as she is influenced by
others and godly wisdom as she is looked to for influence;
flavor her every word, and provide her the favor of those in
her midst.*

*Give her the ability to embrace your freedom and relief from
her sin so she can live life to its fullest—better serving herself
and her family, and most important, glorifying you. Provide her
tools, people, and your Word that she might fortify herself to be
the woman of God you long for. Keep her confident. Keep her
courageous. Keep her positive. Keep her humble. Keep her close.*

*In the name of your Son, Jesus Christ, who develops, fortifies,
and sustains us for his glory. Amen.*

YOUR CARE LABEL

YOU HAVE A CARE LABEL; it's stitched on your heart. But it's not going to do you much good if you don't remember what the instructions say or if you don't take time to reread the label every now and then.

God's Word provides you everything you need to know about the best way to refresh yourself to last a lifetime. If one of the verses below speaks to your heart and renews your spirit, commit it to memory. Cut it out and tape it to your mirror, or better yet, place it where you probably spend most of your time—between the 10:00 and 2:00 position on your steering wheel.

These care instructions are for a gentle spirit—one that isn't bothered by a little agitation—to keep you as glorious as you are at this moment for years to come.

I know the LORD is always with me. I will not be shaken, for he is right beside me. . . . You will show me the way of life, granting me the joy of your presence and the pleasures of living with you forever. **PSALM 16:8, 11**

As he thinks in his heart, so is he. **PROVERBS 23:7, NKJV**

So the creation of the heavens and the earth and everything in them was completed. On the seventh day God had finished his work of creation, so he rested from all his work. **GENESIS 2:1-2**

Guard your heart above all else, for it determines the course of your life. **PROVERBS 4:23**

41

In the same way, husbands ought to love their wives as they love their own bodies. For a man who loves his wife actually shows love for himself. **EPHESIANS 5:28**

Don't worry about anything; instead, pray about everything. Tell God what you need, and thank him for all he has done. **PHILIPPIANS 4:6**

The faithful love of the LORD never ends! His mercies never cease. Great is his faithfulness; his mercies begin afresh each morning. **LAMENTATIONS 3:22-23**

We will no longer be immature like children. We won't be tossed and blown about by every wind of new teaching. We will not be influenced when people try to trick us with lies so clever they sound like the truth. **EPHESIANS 4:14**

As iron sharpens iron, so a friend sharpens a friend. **PROVERBS 27:17**

Those who trust in the LORD will find new strength. They will soar high on wings like eagles. They will run and not grow weary. They will walk and not faint. **ISAIAH 40:31**

I am dying from grief; my years are shortened by sadness. Sin has drained my strength; I am wasting away from within. **PSALM 31:10**

He lets me rest in green meadows; he leads me beside peaceful streams. He renews my strength. **PSALM 23:2-3**

I also pray that you will understand the incredible greatness of God's power for us who believe him. This is the same mighty power that raised Christ from the dead and seated him in the place of honor at God's right hand in the heavenly realms. **EPHESIANS 1:19-20**

Their lives became full of every kind of wickedness, sin, greed, hate, envy, murder, quarreling, deception, malicious behavior, and gossip. **ROMANS 1:29**

Thank you for making me so wonderfully complex! Your workmanship is marvelous—how well I know it.   **PSALM 139:14**

He makes the whole body fit together perfectly. As each part does its own special work, it helps the other parts grow, so that the whole body is healthy and growing and full of love.
EPHESIANS 4:16

Let your conversation be always full of grace, seasoned with salt, so that you may know how to answer everyone.
COLOSSIANS 4:6, NIV

The LORD will guide you continually, giving you water when you are dry and restoring your strength. You will be like a well-watered garden, like an ever-flowing spring.   **ISAIAH 58:11**

Lord, Have Mercy ON MY SOUL

AN ACCOUNTING OF OUR DAYS

OVER THE PAST SEVEN DAYS, I SPENT:

- Forty-two hours at the office. (I'm still waiting for the day when the owner gets to work a twenty-hour workweek.)
- Four hours standing on one leg. Well, not really. But it felt like I did. I actually did invest four hours practicing yoga.
- Three hours futzing with my hair. It's a new cut, and I'm learning to blow it dry, per my stylist, in a more "relevant" style. Hmm . . . I think that was a slam.
- Two hours putting on and refreshing makeup. Surprise! The older you get, the longer it takes because there are way more steps with the eyebrows.
- One hour taking it off. Because of all the stuff I now have to put on my eyebrows.

I could go on and on, but I'd bore you stiff with the extremely temporal things in which I invest my time. So let's consider the time I spent in "deep" thought:

- Twenty hours pondering the state of our country and its leadership. If it's not this, it's the state of our society or something else. It's always something with me.
- Seven hours noodling over noodles. Not *just* noodles, but researching and planning "What's for dinner?"

- One hour wondering what I'm going to wear. And I always wear pretty much the same thing.

I spent the remaining hours of the week sleeping, thinking about our kids (yes, even though they're grown), or considering numerous mindless topics.

How much time did I invest over the past seven days on issues of the soul?

- Twenty-one hours in God's Word. To be honest, this is more than the norm; thanks to you and writing this book, I'm way above my average quota.
- Zero hours thinking about eternity and the state of my soul. *Not good, Ellen.*

Judge not, lest ye be judged. How many hours did *you* spend this week thinking about eternity and the condition of *your* soul? Yep. That's what I thought.

And that's why this chapter made its way into this book. As moms, we're so busy "doing" and thinking about everything else in this world that we rarely carve out time to consider the state of our faith and "life after" all this crazy fun is over.

What do you benefit if you gain the whole world but lose your own soul? MARK 8:36

So let's focus our time on our souls, sister (even though hair products are incredibly fascinating).

WHAT YOU DON'T WORRY ABOUT THAT YOU SHOULD

IN THE FIRST SECTION, "Renew My Spirit," we touched on what we worry about that we shouldn't.

I have been a mother for nearly forty years, so I have a pretty good idea of what you fret about today, and I know what you will likely worry about in the future, especially as it relates to your family. I can tell you not to agonize about *everything*, but I know that sometimes you will, even if you have great faith. I also realize that some of us are just worriers. So if we're gonna worry, let's worry about something we can actually do something about: the state and trajectory of our spiritual growth.

Worry about our spiritual growth, you might ask? Doesn't our spiritual growth just sort of happen? Let me answer it this way: Does your fanny just magically get firmer with each passing year? Probably not. It's something you invest time and energy into improving (or at least maintaining). And results don't happen overnight!

Unlike a perked posterior, our maturation in our walk with Christ will actually do something for us when the dark clouds of a crisis begin to gather. Although we worry about hundreds of little things that might go wrong, we really can't imagine anything tragic happening to our families. Whether it's naiveté or denial, it's difficult to envision our families being in turmoil after the wake of a storm. But trials come to everyone, and we need to be ready.

"The time for us to decide our life priorities is before they are tested," says author and Christian scholar Jim Denison. "Only then can we be ready for challenges when they come. And make no mistake, challenges are coming."[7] It's safe to say that the moment when we are dealing with a personal crisis is not the best time to build our spiritual stamina; rather, it's the time to rely on the stamina we've already developed.

Without my mature faith, I would have gone mad while Scott was missing for three and a half years. His methamphetamine addiction was a storm I never expected to have to ride out. Without my conviction that God had our backs, I would not have made it through those years of failed attempts at rehab, Steve's monthly calls to the morgue, or Scott's shocking return and our long road back to rebuilding his health and our relationship. My faith had been seeded, watered, and fertilized *daily* for thirty-eight years before our baby was lost to the dark world of drugs. If I had just begun to till the soil as the crisis set in, my seed of faith would have been blown away by the storm of fear.

Your soul, sister, needs to be cultivated—now.

> As they sailed across, Jesus settled down for a nap. But soon a fierce storm came down on the lake. The boat was filling with water, and they were in real danger. The disciples went and woke him up, shouting, "Master, Master, we're going to drown!" When Jesus woke up, he rebuked the wind and the raging waves. Suddenly the storm stopped and all was calm. Then he asked them, "Where is your faith?" LUKE 8:23-25

To tend to our souls, we must purposefully invest time to learn intimately of God's promises to us. And there's no better way to do that than to be in a small Bible study group, which provides structure and accountability to stay in the Word. Whether it is a ladies-only study or one you attend with your husband, studying provides knowledge. Knowledge begets wisdom. Wisdom begets faith. And faith begets peace, especially when the storm clouds gather.

UPPING OUR GAME

LAST WEEK DURING ONE of my yoga sessions (as each of us stood on one leg with the other perched against our thigh), the instructor began calling out various other poses: "If you're at level one, stay where you are. Level twos—grab the sole of your perched foot and straighten your leg. Level threes, grab your heel and raise your leg vertically. Level fours . . ." I have no recollection of what he said after that, because I was shocked to learn, after all this time, that there were yoga "levels," and I had no idea which level I belonged to!

In yoga, as in many other areas of life, progression is the name of the game. It's how we know that what we're investing in or what we're doing is working. It's an accounting or measurement of our growth, which is not only good for us—it often becomes an inspiration to others. I found a parallel between upping my game in yoga and advancing my spiritual development.

To progress in yoga, one has to be committed to coming to class; frequency is key. I hit a class two to three times a week, but I also practice various poses and stretches on my own during my "home days." If we want to progress in our understanding of Christ, we, again, must commit to show up. We can't attend a Bible study class or worship service occasionally (or worse, rarely) and expect to advance. Nor can we ignore our quiet time at home when we pray and read Scripture. To grow in our faith, we have to invest time.

The experience of the yoga instructor matters, and it matters a lot. My instructor continues his own education, and rather than just leading a class, he really teaches it. In addition, he actively participates in the poses with us, unlike some leaders who call out poses as they walk around. Those who instruct us in the teaching of Christ must not only be wise to dispense the Word of God, but they should also practice what they teach. I learn best from a leader who "walks the walk" with me.

When I'm in yoga class, I'm "all in." I don't cheat on poses but instead put my all into every move. I sweat like a stuck hog and, sister, I feel the burn. We must be dedicated to our spiritual maturation too. When we're willing to go deep in our study, we may be uncomfortable at times, convicted by what we're learning, but in the end we will find our souls burning for him.

There are women in my yoga class who inspire me. They are graceful. Limber. Strong. Focused. Technically precise. I watch them as they contort into pretzel-like shapes; they make me better and motivate me to work harder and return to class often, so that one day I can achieve their level of mastery. There are also women in my Bible study who inspire me to dig deeper into God's Word, to ask questions to discern his direction and calling for me. Great Christian role models keep us accountable and on the path to improvement.

As disciples of Christ, we must take seriously the progression of our spiritual maturation. As in the practice of yoga, there is no "maintaining" when it comes to our faith walk; our spiritual development is either advancing or declining. And rest assured, someone is watching for someone like you to inspire her to live a godly life.

Practice these things, immerse yourself in them, so that all may see your progress. 1 TIMOTHY 4:15, ESV

Now, wrap your leg around your head and open up your Bible to the book of Hebrews.

ATTENTION DEFICIT PRAYERS

FATHER, I COME BEFORE YOU . . . *Did I put the kids' dentist appointments on the calendar? . . .* Father, I come before you, praising you . . . *I wonder what happened at PTA last night . . .* I humbly lift . . . *I can't believe my mother said that to me . . .* I humbly lift my friend Emma to you; please comfort her . . . *I have to remember to pick up milk after car pool today . . .* Lord, please watch over Emma. Amen.

I am ashamed to admit that this is how some of my prayers go. I am communing with God Almighty, and my mind wanders to milk. What must he think of me and my ADD prayers? If I had a conversation like this with a girlfriend, she'd hang up the phone!

Praise God he doesn't. He stays on the line. But that doesn't let me off the hook.

I don't suffer from actual ADD, which is a serious condition for many people. However, when I can't clear my mind long enough to get through a three-minute prayer with my God, I am showing him disrespect. Hmm . . . that puts a different spin on multitasking, doesn't it? After realizing I struggle to stay focused during my prayer time, I've found a few things that can help us avoid ADD prayers.

Write out your prayers. Whether I write in longhand or type, this exercise helps me think carefully about my praises and petitions to God. Not only is writing out prayers revealing, but as you look back over them, sometimes years later, you will be blessed to see God's provision and your own spiritual growth. You may also be humbled to see how infrequently you simply praise him. Keeping a record of your prayers can be instructional *and* convicting.

Pray Scripture. At times I am not sure how to pray—either for myself or for others. This is when I turn to a Scripture that relates to the need. Frequently, I realize I should be praying Jesus' own prayer (with my commentary in parentheses):

> Our Father in heaven, hallowed be your name, *(I praise you, the one, holy, true God!)*
> your kingdom come, your will be done, on earth as it is in heaven. *(I surrender my will to yours; you know best.)*
> Give us today our daily bread. *(Thank you for providing me all I need.)*
> And forgive us our debts, as we also have forgiven our debtors. *(I am humbled to be forgiven, and I commit to forgive others.)*
> And lead us not into temptation, but deliver us from the evil one. *(Protect and strengthen me so I may avoid sin.)*
> **MATTHEW 6:9-13, NIV**

The Lord's Prayer is like the superstore of prayers!

Last, pray with *someone.* If you've ever been in a crisis, you know the power of someone praying over you. During the years that Scott was missing, I couldn't pray for entire weeks at a time. I was completely prayed out! When I shared the condition of my soul, a woman in my Bible study said, "Ellen, stop praying. Rest. I'm standing in the gap for you." What a relief! It was a blessing unlike any other I had received. To this day, when I sense a sister is "prayed out," I offer to stand in the gap for her.

> Accept my prayer as incense offered to you, and
> my upraised hands as an evening offering. **PSALM 141:2**

We are powerless without powerful prayer, so let's get our ADD under control.

NEW SHADES

I was so excited to pick up my new pair of prescription sunglasses. These glamorous shades would bring me as close to an Audrey Hepburn look as I would ever get.

After the technician made a quick adjustment, I tried on the glasses and realized right away that my vision was a little wa-wa; I could see, but something was different. I told myself that I simply needed time to get accustomed to the prescription and walked out of the store—catching myself as I nearly fell. Hmm . . .

While driving home, I realized that if I closed one eye, my vision cleared up. But when I had both eyes open, the horizon seemed to give off a sort of heat shimmer. Two weeks later I returned the glasses to learn the prescription had been filled incorrectly.

My memory vision—what I see in my childhood rearview mirror—has been known to be wa-wa too, particularly in the way I see my mom. For years, as I drove further and further away from my childhood, I viewed my less-than-perfect growing-up years through the wrong lenses, which made everything appear distorted. Mirages appeared: I recalled experiences not always the way they actually happened, but only as I, as a child, could make sense of them. Distant objects were stretched: The decisions my mother made that seemed horrific then (and even years later) were likely the only arrangements that could have been made at the time.

As a young mother, lovingly doting on my wee babies, I became incensed at my mom and what she'd put me through. I wrestled with her decisions during a long period of estrangement. But I praise God that, as the years progressed, he showed me that I needed new lenses with which to view my childhood: lenses that included seeing the blessing that resulted from some of the tragedy. The night before my mom died, I had the sweetest (and most normal) conversation I had ever had with her. At the time, she was very ill, but no one thought she was on her deathbed. Yet that night she died peacefully in her sleep, making our last conversation one of the most precious gifts I've ever received.

If, like mine, your mom had "challenges," you might also tend to remember only her hurtful or flat-out wrong parenting. Your memory vision may be clouded by years of tears or times of "seeing red" because of her poor choices. *I truly understand.* But to find the abundant life Jesus promised (see John 10:10, ESV), you might have to don new shades to look past the wrong and see what was right in that mess: God was and is preparing you for his glory— as well as your own.

> The Holy Spirit prays for us with groanings that cannot be expressed in words. And the Father who knows all hearts knows what the Spirit is saying, for the Spirit pleads for us believers in harmony with God's own will. *And we know that God causes everything to work together for the good of those who love God and are called according to his purpose for them.* For God knew his people in advance, and he chose them to become like his Son, so that his Son would be the firstborn among many brothers and sisters.

And having chosen them, he called them to come to him. And having called them, he gave them right standing with himself. *And having given them right standing, he gave them his glory.* ROMANS 8:26-30, EMPHASIS MINE

We hate to admit it, but we often become kinder, gentler, more thoughtful people as the result of our trials. And praise God, our kids will be better because of the fire they've walked through too. Let's just hope they're willing to buy some new shades when they're grown and look back on their childhood.

PRAY THIS, NOT THAT

THE DAY I STARTED WRITING this section, I received a very troubling call at the office: Our agency had been underbid for a sizable job. But this was not a typical account.

We had an existing relationship with this client and had built a highly specialized team of experts to serve them. These team members were so uniquely trained for this type of work that they worked only on this account. Moving them into other positions in our company was not an option. You see my heartbreak.

The surprising news hit us very hard, especially when the client told us how much they loved working with us because of the outstanding quality and exceptional service we had consistently delivered for four years. But their budgets had been cut, and they had been directed to save money. The competing bid was so much lower that we couldn't even begin to counter it.

So Steve (that wonderful husband of mine is also my brilliant business partner) and I have been doing what we have learned to do when a resolution is unclear: We pray for faith, rather than a fix.

While a quick fix would sure help me sleep better at night, I've learned that relying on God and trusting him completely always results in solutions I could have never imagined. He has shown us time and time again that the blessing is often in what comes "next" rather than in our pea-size solution for the moment. But sometimes it's not easy to stay the course.

My mind urges me to pray, *Fix this, Lord! Restore our business!* But my soul knows from a lifetime of walking with him that God's ways are higher than my ways. He knows what blessings are in store for us and our employees that I cannot even begin to imagine.

Whenever you are faced with a challenge or crisis, try praying for faith rather than your version of the fix. Join Steve and me as we pray, "Lord, give us faith. Help us to stand firm in the hope you offer us and to remember your promise of knowing our every need. Let us not waver. Keep us courageous. Give us wisdom. Thank you for your provision today and in the days to come."

I do believe, but help me overcome my unbelief! **MARK 9:24**

Steve and I don't yet know how our work situation will play out. We are keeping the lines of communication with our client open, and we hope to hit on a solution that works for everyone. I believe, whatever the outcome, God will bless our company. But I tell you, sister, some hours my faith is stronger than others. Yours too?

WISE, RICH, OR THIN. PICK TWO.

IN PROJECT MANAGEMENT, there is a philosophy summed up by this saying: "Fast, good, or cheap. Pick two." Everyone wants a quality product or service, but it can rarely be developed both on a short timeline and at a low cost. A product can often be created quickly, but the speed of development often results in increased overhead and higher cost. Or it can be cranked out quickly and less expensively, but it will likely be a stinker. The point is, pick your goals carefully or you might not get the one that is most important to you.

If I were to challenge you to choose between investing in becoming wise, rich, or thin, which two would you opt for? Closer to home: Which two do you invest more time in developing today? No shocker here. Even good churchgoing girls like us chase rich and thin most often. Not many of us are pursuing the thing that counts most when it comes to our souls.

Some women say they are not interested in being rich, and that is true. Many of us could care less about our family's net worth; it's what we can purchase with money to gain prestige for ourselves or our children that drives us. Some of us will spend our last dime in an attempt to repair broken trust or a damaged relationship through the purchase of gifts. My challenge was investing in multiple programs to cure our son's addiction. It's not that the programs were ineffective. The problem was our timing: Scott was not ready to be saved from himself.

Steve and I found that money couldn't buy Scott sobriety. The thousands of dollars we spent didn't end his addiction. Our son will tell you he is sober only by the grace of God. For those of us who think we'll be happier or can make our problems go away with just a little more money, I think Solomon nailed it: "Those who love money will never have enough" (Ecclesiastes 5:10).

Many of us fall to our culture's definition of beauty and chase attributes that are hilariously evasive. We can shoot up with all the Botox in the world, but we're not going to catch our youth again. We might lose a few pounds, but I'll bet you my taco that we'll never lose them in the areas we most want to; that perfect body is pure fantasy. My beauty obsession is my hair: It's baby fine and straight as a board. Do you know how many products I have bought striving for a mane that rivals those on the models in the Pantene ads? Guess what? No matter what I put in my hair, it is still baby fine and straight as a board.

The most beautiful women I know are not thin. They are not wrinkle-free. They don't sport Cindy Crawford–like tresses. The most beautiful women I know and admire have established a unique style "within." The reflection in your mirror might make you feel good today, but it won't be much comfort when you need godly insight.

So what if we race after rich and thin but fail to invest anything to become wise?

Our money and prestige can be wiped out by Wall Street tomorrow. Our beauty will fade—I don't care how often you hit the gym or how many products you buy. Only wisdom can provide us insight so that we might grow in our knowledge of God (Ephesians 1:17), and that knowledge will bring peace to our souls when we need it most (James 3:17).

> If you need wisdom, ask our generous God, and he will give it to you. **JAMES 1:5**

Wise, rich, or thin. Pick carefully.

IT'S SOMETHING ALL THE TIME

AVA HAS A FAVORITE DOLL NAMED VIOLET. Her maternal instinct is strong; even at the tender age of ten months she rocked, patted, and cooed at her baby doll. For years, if you saw Ava, you knew Violet was nearby.

One evening when Ava was about three, she entered the kitchen carrying Violet as Shauna prepared dinner. Striking up a conversation, Shauna asked casually how many babies Ava thought she would have. "Oh!" answered Ava as she waved her arms and rolled her eyes. "I'm not having babies. With these kids, it's something all the time."

No duh. That's been my experience too. But I've also discovered that blessings are often wrapped in those "somethings."

Our first "something" with Scott occurred one evening when he came to Steve and me ready to discuss with us his sexual orientation. We weren't surprised; we had suspected Scott was gay since he was young. For years, I worried how he would manage bullies as he entered high school and what his future would look like, and I prayed that somehow "this cup would pass from him." I knew my church pastors and Christian friends didn't condone homosexuality—but given what I saw in my son, I sometimes resented the ease with which they downplayed the struggle of those who identified as gay.

So when Scott was finally ready to open his heart to us, our words weren't condemning but were rooted in our unconditional love for him. The tears and look of relief on that child's face reassured me that, as hard as this was, God had blessed me with a child who knew he was loved. I might not have understood or approved of everything Scott did, but I wanted him to know I would always cherish him.

Several years later, Scott disappeared. Search as we may, we couldn't find him; he was missing for more than three years. For many months, we agonized that he wasn't even alive. On the day he returned, we thanked God that he was alive, but within hours of his homecoming he told us he was HIV positive. Over the next few days we learned the depth of his drug addiction and what he was facing in his battle to kick meth. This is a lot of "somethings" with one kid.

Learning he was infected with HIV was crushing, but we knew the disease could be treated. My perspective of his diagnosis was very different from what it might have been; after all, just the week before I'd thought my child was dead! God blessed me with a virtual loss to lessen the blow.

Scott's conviction to stay sober these past nine years has taught me so much about fortitude. Scott struggled as a young man to fight his demons; God has blessed me to see him today as a strong, loving, and kind man.

As moms, we think these "somethings" are disasters. And at the moment we're going through them, they often are. But, sweet sister, there's dancing on the other side.

> You have turned my mourning into joyful dancing. You have taken away my clothes of mourning and clothed me with joy, that I might sing praises to you and not be silent. O LORD my God, I will give you thanks forever! **PSALM 30:11-12**

Yep. It's something all the time. I thank God for that. Without the "somethings," I'd never know how incredibly blessed I am.

THE TUG OF TRUTHS

WHILE I DON'T HAVE THE HONOR of knowing you or your sweet family, I do know that your faith and those truths you hold most dear will be tested. If your kiddos are young, you may not have an inkling of how it will come down, but for sure the game will be played.

Believe it or not, just as your parents relinquished control of you, you will be required to do the same for your kids. And never is it harder than when you see your adult children making decisions you know are disastrous or at least detrimental to their well-being. Sometimes your children will invite you into conversations to counsel and pray. But sometimes they will not.

At such times, you will get on your knees, and you will hold on to your truth. But be careful of holding on to whatever truth you believe too tightly; there's another truth, that of unconditional love, that is pulling on the other end of the rope.

I've visited with Christian moms who've struggled with their child's sexual identity. Many are relieved to hear from another Christian that homosexuality is not the unpardonable sin. Rejecting them or not loving them would be as much a sin. I've watched a friend of mine support her child who was on trial for a serious crime; her example of holding on to her rope of unconditional love as she felt the pull of disappointment and shame moved me. Those of us who are parents of addicts or recovering addicts do not dismiss the trail of destruction, broken lives, and lawlessness left in the wake of our children's terrible choices but hold on tightly to any thread that can pull them back to us. Unconditional love doesn't mean we accept the behavior or lifestyle our child has adopted, but it does require living the witness that Christ set before us. And what big sandals those are to fill.

That is why it is critical for you to know *all* of God's Word, not just the tightly held beliefs that resonate with you for the moment. Be patient with yourself and others as the Holy Spirit reveals wrong attitudes or actions and convicts you. It takes time to come to grips with the concept that showing unconditional love always trumps pointing out or judging someone else's sin.

> Love is patient and kind. Love is not jealous or boastful or proud or rude. It does not demand its own way. It is not irritable, and it keeps no record of being wronged. It does not rejoice about injustice but rejoices whenever the truth wins out. Love never gives up, never loses faith, is always hopeful, and endures through every circumstance.
> 1 CORINTHIANS 13:4-7

Unconditional love is rarely easy. It will be tested. Hold on to your rope.

day 28

ONE TOO MANY BROWNIES

STEVE LOVES SWEETS. When I came across an Ina Garten recipe for brownies that called for (among other decadent ingredients) a pound of butter, six eggs, more than two pounds of chocolate, three cups of walnuts, and only a little more than a cup of flour, I thought, *How could this not be marvelous?*

Once the brownies were out of the oven and cooled, the recipe instructed me to refrigerate them until they were chilled. Steve could hardly wait. Finally, we pulled them out to sample. After we'd cut off two small bites and popped them into our mouths, we locked eyes. Oh. My. Goodness. That was a mistake.

Needless to say, they were heavenly. I decided to cut a few more brownies.

We had one. Then another. And then I thought I was going to barf.

Did I not know what went into the brownies?
Yes, I did. I knew exactly what I was downing.

Did I think this was a good idea at the time?
No. I knew this was a bad idea, but reasoning didn't
    win out.

Did I seek to extend pleasure from the first brownie to
    the second and third?

Absolutely. If one was that good, numbers two and three should be divine!

Did I regret having the second and third helpings?
Yes. I was very remorseful (but only after my stomach started to rebel).

Will I do it again?
Probably. The brownies are *really* good.

And there lies my problem, sisters. I'm weak and not always smart.

Portion control can be a bit of a challenge for many of us, and it's not just dessert that we indulge in. Just look in our closets, our homes, our garages, our attics. Even our schedules are bulging with excess. We often look to things, activities, and sometimes even people for the pleasure and contentment that only God can provide.

If you have portion control issues too, join me in this prayer when you're about to take your next serving, purchase your next item, or schedule your next outing: *Lord, fill me with you.*

"The LORD is my portion," says my soul, "therefore I will hope in him." **LAMENTATIONS 3:24, ESV**

I feel better already. (And I'm not going near those brownies tonight.)

RECLAIMING OUR HOLY DAYS

MY HEART BREAKS for what Christmas has become and for what Easter represents to so many. When considering these two most holy seasons of celebration, our Christian witness as a whole has gone to pot. Santas and Easter bunnies—not anticipation and repentance as we wait for a returning King—are now the primary symbols of these holidays.

Consider, in contrast, the way committed Jews celebrate Yom Kippur, the holiest day on the Jewish calendar (and one of the High Holy Days along with Rosh Hashanah). Also known as the "Day of Atonement," this is a day dedicated to repentance and spiritual growth through prayer by the Jewish community throughout the world.

> "It shall be a sacred occasion for you: You shall practice self-denial" (Leviticus 23:27). Fasting is seen as fulfilling this biblical commandment. . . .
> Yom Kippur is the moment in Jewish time when we dedicate our mind, body, and soul to reconciliation with God, our fellow human beings, and ourselves. . . . On this journey we are both seekers and givers of pardon.[8]

Self-denial? How can they possibly have a holiday without gifts, food, and bins of decorations?

Or consider how devout Muslims observe Ramadan. During the ninth month of the Islamic calendar, millions of Muslims dedicate *an entire month* to daylight fasting, prayer, service, and various other areas of self-denial with the sole purpose of rededicating themselves to their faith.

An entire month! I can't make it from Christmas brunch to Christmas dinner without a snack. And not once on Christmas Day have I opened my Bible.

This is not about Christians trying to impress their neighbors with extreme acts of self-deprivation. One of the hallmarks of Christianity, in fact, is that we are saved by grace, not works. But shouldn't our gratitude for what God has done for us be seen in the way we honor him on our holiest days? Instead, Christmas has become an orgy of food, parties, and gifts. Even some Christian families are so exhausted that they don't make it to a Christmas Eve service. Prayer? Oh yes. We say one right before we eat. News flash: This was the day *our Savior* was born. We all act like it's *our* birthday. Hmm . . . what's wrong with this picture?

Most Christians show a bit more reverence toward Easter, considered our holiest of holidays. (I think that may be because the secular world is a little afraid to mess with it. Can I hear an "Amen, hallelujah!"?) Even so, sometime over the past century, the Easter bunny has hopped onto the scene with baskets filled with "cool stuff." Of course there are also eggs to dye, hide, and hunt, as well as hams to bake and eggs to devil. Church service? Oh yes. We make it to church. But pray, repent, read Scripture, and forgive others during our holy week? No. Can't. We're on spring break vacation.

I hope that you, as my sisters in Christ, will help me. We have got to turn the world's eyes away from Target and the grocery store in order to see the glory of the Father, Son, and Holy Spirit.

> As obedient children, do not conform to the evil desires you had when you lived in ignorance. But just as he who called you is holy, so be holy in all you do; for it is written: "Be holy, because I am holy." **1 PETER 1:14-16, NIV**

Santa hijacked Christmas. Some crazy rabbit ran off with Easter. Let's ransom our Holy Days and take them back as our own.

DON'T DO IT FOR THE KIDS

WE WENT TO BOTH Disneyland and Disney World for the kids. We made multiple trips to the zoo, and for years we rode roller coasters at Six Flags Over Texas. We took in a wide variety of water parks, including one with a natural-fed spring that made us feel as if we were slipping into a slushy. We did all of this for our kids.

What we didn't do was go to church for them. We went to church for us.

I visited with a woman recently who shared with me that she didn't enjoy going to church. I think she said it was boring. When I asked her why they continued to go, she said, "We do it for the kids." Hmm . . .

Going to church for the kids is like feeding them gummy bears and Kool-Aid while you sit and starve. Neither of you will get the nourishment you need.

When you settle for getting nothing out of the sermon and fail to connect to the almighty God, you end up famished. If there's anything positive about the experience for the kids, it's likely just a sugarcoated shell.

To raise our children in a God-honoring Christian home, Steve and I had to feed our own souls first. We needed to attend a church that felt like home. We needed outstanding sermons that challenged us to learn. We needed music that moved us to worship. We needed a small group to hold us accountable and to connect us with other believers whom we in turn could love on. We needed teachers to guide us in our studies and show us how to apply what we learned.

We had to be intrigued. We had to be challenged—intellectually and spiritually. We needed to be in an environment where we could "open" ourselves to the Word of God.

To lead our children, we had to first be led.

As the kids grew older, youth programs and camps were important and kept them involved, but it was those sermons that we heard together as a family that were discussed over Sunday lunch. And it was those messages that built our foundation and insight into God's faithful love that carried us all when we needed it the most.

> The Lord says, "These people say they are mine. They honor me with their lips, but their hearts are far from me. And their worship of me is nothing but man-made rules learned by rote." ISAIAH 29:13

Our children will not be able to vouch for us at the pearly gates. Worship from the heart, not just the lips. And don't go to church for the kids.

BACK FROM THE DEAD

SPORTING A PAIR OF PIGTAILS and my favorite red Keds, I held my dad's hand as we exited the post office, and that's when I noticed a big commotion across the street. Now it's important to note that in that one-traffic-light town, any type of activity would cause a stir. But this looked real exciting. When I asked my dad what was going on, he said, "They're putting up a tent for our revival."

What? I'd been going to church all my life, so I certainly knew what a revival was: A revival was church—every single night of the week for six nights during the summer (when I really wanted to be home playing with the neighborhood kids), preached by a visiting pastor (who typically went on and on and on). Trust me: Getting through that week every summer was more like *survival* than revival to me.

This was something new. Church in a tent? Well, that was the craziest thing I had ever heard in my eight years of walking on this earth. Why in the world would we sit outside *in July, in Texas*, when we had a perfectly good air-conditioned church?

But just a couple of days later, to that tent we trekked. I have to admit, as we entered I was a little excited about getting to worship outside, and I really got worked up when they handed out these little fans so we could keep ourselves cool. Oh, this was something fresh and new all right. My own personal fan. I went to town with that baby; it was like a "blue norther" (that's Southern speak for a cold front) was blowing down our row.

Something else fresh and new was blowing in that week, and that was God's Word. The guest pastor came from a neighboring town, and he was dynamic, witty, and direct. He engaged us. He entertained us. And he convicted us. Well, not me. I hadn't gotten a full grasp on my sinful nature yet. But he got my parents' attention.

On our short drive home, Mom and Dad's conversation was lively but serious. I remember Mom saying, "I needed a revival and didn't even know it." As they discussed the message and its application to their lives, I didn't understand the details, but I got the big picture: A revival wasn't an event we attended, it was something that happened deep in the soul. I listened and watched as my parents were restored.

We need a revival too. We need to be reminded of the wonder of God. We need to be restored by his grace, mercy, and forgiveness. We need a renewed confidence in the power of redemption from our sin. We need a revival of repentance to turn from our petty sins of gossip, jealousy, envy, and pride. We need our hearts and souls to be brought back from the dead so we may rightfully, and with joy, accept our place in his Kingdom. Sister, we need to open our hearts and minds as we head to the tent of revival to hear a fresh word from God.

The high and lofty one who lives in eternity, the Holy One, says this: "I live in the high and holy place with those whose spirits are contrite and humble. I restore the crushed spirit of the humble and revive the courage of those with repentant hearts." ISAIAH 57:15

That summer revival ended later that week, as always, with one final round of "Amazing Grace." I was happy for my parents, knowing something had changed. But I was really happy for me. Night six ended with homemade ice cream. Amen!

GO SHOPPING

WHEN I SHOP FOR CLOTHES, I do so with laser-like focus to find just the right pieces. Steve and I are the same way when we shop for a church. Some of our church shopping was prompted by physical moves of our address; others were prompted by the moving of the Holy Spirit. Because of my vast church-shopping experience, I would love to share with you what I've learned in case you're ever in the market too:

Online shopping is of little use. Christian church websites are only slightly informative: "We love Jesus, we serve, we care . . . blah, blah, blah." They are good places to find out the worship style (traditional or contemporary) and service times. From there, we have to "hit the dressing room," aka the sanctuary, and try it on for size.

Theology matters. Does the urging of the Holy Spirit tell us that we align with the faith and practice? The various theologies among different denominations and churches can be confusing, but it's critical that our churches be Bible based and Christ centered. To get to their core tenets, we should meet with the clergy or other church leaders. If we disagree, we move on. The rest of the checklist is useless if this doesn't "fit."

Look for the right worship style. Traditional or contemporary? Be sure the style of worship attracts you to God rather than distracts you from him. He wants you in an atmosphere where you can speak to him and, most important, where you can hear him speak to you. When your heart starts beating so loudly that you're sure the person next to you can hear it, that's the Holy Spirit. Congratulations, you may have found it! You look radiant in that pew!

Be challenged. Spiritual maturation occurs one day at a time and often in our personal time with the Lord, but deeper learning is achieved when we're led by exceptional pastors and teachers. Steve and I know we have found "our home" when we talk about the sermon or the lesson on our way home. Of course, powerful messages are sometimes convicting, so the fit may be very uncomfortable at first. The longer you wear it, though, the better it feels.

Geography is a consideration. I'm good with the occasional "skip" on Sunday to enjoy a Sabbath with your family over pancakes. But that's occasional. You and your family must get *in the groove* of being in worship. I know many faithful attenders who drive forty-five minutes to church. I applaud them and would do the same if necessary, but Steve and I have found our attendance is more regular when our church is in our community.

Look for a place to serve. Church is not entertainment, nor is it a spectator event. To reap the greatest benefit, we must sow seeds of service. Once you've settled into your new church home, start looking for a place to serve. We all come in and out of seasons of service, but mostly we're called to be in. All in.

Ignore imperfections. We inspect a garment for flaws before we buy it, but we can't do this at church. Any church is about as imperfect an institution as there ever was. Because every church is filled with sinners who care *a lot* about *everything*, there's going to be dissension. A little pull or snag is to be expected.

Let us not neglect our meeting together, as some people do, but encourage one another, especially now that the day of his return is drawing near. **HEBREWS 10:25**

Shopping for new pieces to augment your wardrobe may take a few weeks. Shopping for a church might take months—but the reward will last you and your family through eternity. If you haven't yet found your church home, start shopping!

IT'S NOT ALGEBRA

You're making this harder than it is.

Night after night as I sat with the kids doing homework at the kitchen table, I would find myself thinking this. I know I said it out loud at least once to each kid. Both times their math book was open. Both times I was on my last nerve.

Don't you just ache for God as you struggle to learn his truth? Can you imagine how many times he thinks this about us? *Child, it's not this hard. Open your spirit, and let me teach you.*

Just as some kids must surrender, stop grumbling, and get past "I have no idea why I need to learn this and how I'll ever use it," so must we. If we're to progress, God needs us to have teachable spirits.

Some people are born with an open mind and a willingness to be groomed. I've worked with or managed professionals for more than thirty years and have seen the success achieved by those who are teachable. Unfortunately, I have also witnessed the fallout of those unwilling to heed and apply wise counsel. While they were intelligent, ambitious people, this group was stubborn, arrogant, and prideful whenever someone tried to teach them. There's an important lesson here for us as it relates to our surrender to Scripture.

I have been a member of many Bible studies and walked alongside Christian women at all levels of spiritual maturation: from those who didn't know *if* they believed to those who could not remember ever *not* believing. I have watched faith blossom before my very eyes, and I have watched it crash and burn. I realize that those who have failed to learn and grow were often:

Obstinate. They firmly adhered to their own personal truth over God's, especially when his Word grew convicting.

Dismissive. Their conceit led them to look for what was wrong in Christ's teaching, rather than what was instructive.

Egotistical. Their self-interest, intellect, and comfort in this world trumped all other direction. Especially God's.

As I sat with my kids at the kitchen table, I asked only that they listen, practice, and review. And that's all Christ asks of us. If you struggle to understand and adopt God's Word, pray for the Holy Spirit to intercede on your behalf. Ask for his help to give you a willing heart and an open, humble mind. Teachable spirits are sometimes developed one lesson at a time.

> Your "wisdom" and "knowledge" have led you astray, and you said, "I am the only one, and there is no other."
> **ISAIAH 47:10**

How teachable are you? Let's not make this harder than it is.

JESUS RIDING SHOTGUN

"THE TWO MOST IMPORTANT DAYS of your life," said Mark Twain, "are the day you were born and the day you found out why."

If you don't know why you were born, I can tell you. You were born for the equipping of the saints. The ones sulking on the couch right now because you insisted they do their chores. (Yes, those little sinners today will be saints tomorrow. I know. It's hard to imagine.)

My first ministry was my kids. Long before launching my career or thinking of writing books, I knew my most important mission field was my children and their friends. Over the years I found that it was always in the mundane that the heavens would open.

Mom, you have a captive audience. Testify.

As they sit at the counter while you spread their PB and J, talk with them about the blessings of God's provision. Our children live very privileged lives, so you must take every opportunity to help them develop a spirit of thanksgiving and gratitude. This will equip your saints with joy.

As you wipe a nose, pat a back, or rock them when they're sick, pray for their healing so they may see your reliance on God. Your children need to hear your petition on their behalf, as well as know the importance of prayer. This will equip your saints with faith.

As they listen to you share with your husband your

frustration with your mom, your job, or a friend, talk about the challenge constructively. Ask them to help you problem solve how you might address the situation in a way that honors Christ. This will equip your saints to bear witness.

As you fill the backseat for your car-pool run, turn off the radio. Listen for opportunities for Jesus to join in. As they get older, you will find the car is the safest place for your kids (and sometimes their friends) to talk to you. I learned that I could get my kids to tell me almost anything in the car because they didn't have to make eye contact. Just make sure Jesus is riding shotgun, and he will help you equip your saints with the knowledge of the gift of salvation.

> He Himself gave some to be apostles, some prophets, some evangelists, and some pastors and teachers, for the equipping of the saints for the work of ministry, for the edifying of the body of Christ. **EPHESIANS 4:11-12, NKJV**

As Christians, you and I are in the soul business. For you, that's a home-based business. Equip your saints.

FIFTY SHADES OF WHITE

AFTER NEARLY TWO YEARS of discussion and design, our home was finally under construction, and it was time to consider exterior paint colors. Since the house is modern, we turned our attention to the "whites." Do you know how many shades of white stucco there are? Or how many more shades they turn when they take on the environment around them? When we were looking, there had to be fifty shades—ranging from a "pinky" white to a "greeny" white. It was maddening. Depending on the season we were in, the time of day, and whether the sky was filled with threatening clouds or radiant sunshine, the colors of stucco samples changed before our eyes; it was almost impossible to tell a real white from a pastel.

Jesus was "true white." His environment did not affect his perfection, even though he continuously surrounded himself with sinners. The calendar didn't influence him either. Regardless of the day, week, or month, nothing interfered with his single-minded goal—to be holy. The time of day didn't influence him; morning, noon, or night, he was consistent in his ministry and his message. Nor did the weather produce any change; whether it was a cloudless day or there were storm clouds on the horizon, he was pure in his peace.

Jesus, the Son of God, remained pure white because he was not conflicted or torn between pleasing the world and glorifying his Father. It's when we begin to lose our single-minded focus on God's glorification that our own white takes on dingy undertones.

I'm not as pure as I would like to be—I'm more off-white. I'm often affected by those around me, taking on the hue of those who are not believers, those who are negative, or those who live in fear. Some of us are affected by the calendar—particularly a week or so each month when the hormones are raging and our white isn't so bright. My white is also often tainted by the time of day—at the end of a long and frustrating workday, I'm definitely more gray than white. The weather can affect me as well—one good personal storm, and my white can become a gloomy blue. These "conditions" detract from my single-minded exaltation of God.

James 4:8 warns us to "wash [our] hands" and "purify [our] hearts, for [our] loyalty is divided between God and the world." James is telling us that if we are not single-mindedly pursuing the glory of God, we will struggle to sustain our faith. Trying to serve two masters, the world and God, will eventually dull our white. To be single-minded is to be loyal to Christ, unashamed and unapologetic for our faith. We are card-carrying, courageous, Bible-toting Christians. And we demonstrate this by loving better, deeper, and wider than anyone sporting fifty shades of gray.

> Everything is pure to those whose hearts are pure. But nothing is pure to those who are corrupt and unbelieving, because their minds and consciences are corrupted. Such people claim they know God, but they deny him by the way they live. TITUS 1:15-16

Let's commit to do our part to whiten our whites.

day 36

IF YOU ONLY REMEMBER THIS

YEARS AGO, my friend Elaine and I found ourselves in a deep discussion about our faith. At one point in the conversation I said, "I can't believe how God has so richly blessed me when I am so bad." As her brows narrowed, she very firmly corrected me, "You're not bad. You're holy."

"Holy? Me? Oh, no. I'm a lot of things, but holy is not one of them."

Oops. I was wrong. If there's one thing I want you to remember, it's this: You are holy. When you chose to follow Christ, you took on a new persona. You traded in your sinner self (the old one that was never convicted and never repented of sin) for your righteous self.

> Put on your new nature, created to be like God—truly righteous and holy. **EPHESIANS 4:24**

This happened without most of us even knowing it! It was sort of like being born: We just appeared here, this way. As his daughters, we are *created* to be like God. Of course, with this new nature, we must accept the charge to choose to *act* holy.

> You must be holy in everything you do, just as God who chose you is holy. For the Scriptures say, "You must be holy because I am holy." **1 PETER 1:15-16**

I'm sometimes lovingly teased by friends who are not devout believers; some sort of straddle the fence, while others are out in the far pasture. When I say something "Christian," they often laugh, shake their heads, and say, "Ellen, you're so good." My knee-jerk reaction is "Oh, no. I'm not good!" I'm not sure whether my reaction is fueled by embarrassment or false humility, but I *am* sure that when I fail to claim my holiness, I subconsciously and indirectly devalue the power of Christ.

> May you always be filled with the fruit of your salvation— the righteous character produced in your life by Jesus Christ—for this will bring much glory and praise to God. **PHILIPPIANS 1:11**

Our good character is a benefit of our salvation and is God's product, not our own. Furthermore, when we act on it so others can see it, we glorify God! But we can't confuse our actions with how we received this crown of glory in the first place:

> People are counted as righteous, not because of their work, but because of their faith in God who forgives sinners. **ROMANS 4:5**

Sister, by faith alone we are holy. Those who don't believe are not holy. So, yes, to some you *are* holier than thou. Own it.

Holy God, we are overjoyed at the gift of your salvation. Thank you, Lord, for welcoming us into your presence.

You know every hair on this sweet woman's head. As she reads this, you know the desires of her heart and the condition of her soul. I pray, Father, that you will keep her single-minded, bold, and courageous as she walks with you.

As she waits patiently and expectantly for a solution, Lord, provide her the tools and willingness she needs to strengthen her faith. When she's at the end of her rope, give her a sign of hope to remedy the pain of her unbelief. Show her how to trust you completely in the face of disaster, and give her grace as she ministers to those who are confronting their own tragedy.

Implant a deep desire and the discipline to take her study and understanding of you to the next level. Give her discernment as she studies your Word, and bless her with the wisdom to apply it.

I know her soul will be challenged in the weeks, months, or years to come as she deals with situations that are confusing or controversial. Give her the ability to love unconditionally for the sake of her own soul and those of other people. Bless her with the ability to extend grace so that she and others will experience the healing power of forgiveness.

Father, I pray you will be blessed by her beautiful shade of white. Remind her that she is virtuous and morally excellent. Press on her heart the truth that she is righteous, pure, and honorable because of you. Let her not forget that she is holy and that when she responds from her new nature, you are glorified.

In the name of the Father, Son, and Holy Ghost, who provides us the most excellent way. Amen.

YOUR SHOPPING LIST

FOR A WOMAN WHO WORKS full-time, I cook a lot.
However, I'm not the type who wakes up on a Wednesday and
says, "Hmm . . . tonight we'll have grilled salmon, steamed
spinach, and roasted purple potatoes." No. In order for me to
prepare a well-balanced, thought-out dinner, I must:

> *Research.* I go online and leaf through cookbooks, look-
> ing for inspiration (otherwise we'd have the same six
> meals in rotation). I love my "quiet time" with my
> recipes on Saturday morning—always a cup of coffee
> in hand and great music playing in the background.
> *Plan.* To cook dinner, especially on a weeknight, I have
> to look ahead at my schedule to predict approxi-
> mately what time we will get home each evening.
> Some nights I have thirty minutes to prepare dinner;
> other nights I have an hour. This information is
> important in order to serve dinner at the optimum
> hour rather than at bedtime!
> *Shop.* After investigating what I have (and don't have)
> in my pantry and fridge, I make my grocery list and
> head to the store(s). Much to the chagrin of my
> shopping partner (Steve), two or more grocery stores
> might be involved.

Then I must chop, stir, simmer, and bake. I can assem-
ble all the best recipes and ingredients in the world, but our
meal will not cook itself. Pots, pans, and a bit of manual
labor are involved. I actually have to *do* it.

Feeding our souls is a little like cooking dinner. I've

attempted to provide you some research and insight. I planned each day's reading to optimize your schedule. And I've prepared a list of ingredients that can nourish you your whole life through. But, sister, only you can do something with them.

What do you benefit if you gain the whole world but lose your own soul? **MARK 8:36**

As they sailed across, Jesus settled down for a nap. But soon a fierce storm came down on the lake. The boat was filling with water, and they were in real danger. The disciples went and woke him up, shouting, "Master, Master, we're going to drown!" When Jesus woke up, he rebuked the wind and the raging waves. Suddenly the storm stopped and all was calm. Then he asked them, "Where is your faith?" **LUKE 8:23-25**

Practice these things, immerse yourself in them, so that all may see your progress. **1 TIMOTHY 4:15, ESV**

Accept my prayer as incense offered to you, and my upraised hands as an evening offering. **PSALM 141:2**

The Holy Spirit prays for us with groanings that cannot be expressed in words. And the Father who knows all hearts knows what the Spirit is saying, for the Spirit pleads for us believers in harmony with God's own will. *And we know that God causes everything to work together for the good of those who love God and are called according to his purpose for them.* For God knew his people in advance, and he chose them to become like his Son, so that his Son would be the firstborn among many brothers and sisters. And having chosen them, he called them to come to him. And having called them, he gave them right standing with himself. *And having given them right standing, he gave them his glory.* **ROMANS 8:26-30, EMPHASIS MINE**

I do believe, but help me overcome my unbelief! **MARK 9:24**

Those who love money will never have enough. ECCLESIASTES 5:10

I pray for you constantly, asking God, the glorious Father of our Lord Jesus Christ, to give you spiritual wisdom and insight so that you might grow in your knowledge of God.
EPHESIANS 1:16-17

But the wisdom from above is first of all pure. It is also peace loving, gentle at all times, and willing to yield to others. It is full of mercy and the fruit of good deeds. It shows no favoritism and is always sincere. JAMES 3:17

If you need wisdom, ask our generous God, and he will give it to you. JAMES 1:5

You have turned my mourning into joyful dancing. You have taken away my clothes of mourning and clothed me with joy, that I might sing praises to you and not be silent. O LORD my God, I will give you thanks forever! PSALM 30:11-12

Love is patient and kind. Love is not jealous or boastful or proud or rude. It does not demand its own way. It is not irritable, and it keeps no record of being wronged. It does not rejoice about injustice but rejoices whenever the truth wins out. Love never gives up, never loses faith, is always hopeful, and endures through every circumstance. 1 CORINTHIANS 13:4-7

"The LORD is my portion," says my soul, "therefore I will hope in him." LAMENTATIONS 3:24, ESV

As obedient children, do not conform to the evil desires you had when you lived in ignorance. But just as he who called you is holy, so be holy in all you do; for it is written: "Be holy, because I am holy." 1 PETER 1:14-16, NIV

The Lord says, "These people say they are mine. They honor me with their lips, but their hearts are far from me. And their worship of me is nothing but man-made rules learned by rote." ISAIAH 29:13

The high and lofty one who lives in eternity, the Holy One, says this: "I live in the high and holy place with those whose spirits are contrite and humble. I restore the crushed spirit of the humble and revive the courage of those with repentant hearts." ISAIAH 57:15

Let us not neglect our meeting together, as some people do, but encourage one another, especially now that the day of his return is drawing near. HEBREWS 10:25

Your "wisdom" and "knowledge" have led you astray, and you said, "I am the only one, and there is no other." ISAIAH 47:10

He Himself gave some to be apostles, some prophets, some evangelists, and some pastors and teachers, for the equipping of the saints for the work of ministry, for the edifying of the body of Christ. EPHESIANS 4:11-12, NKJV

Come close to God, and God will come close to you. Wash your hands, you sinners; purify your hearts, for your loyalty is divided between God and the world. JAMES 4:8

Everything is pure to those whose hearts are pure. But nothing is pure to those who are corrupt and unbelieving, because their minds and consciences are corrupted. Such people claim they know God, but they deny him by the way they live. TITUS 1:15-16

Put on your new nature, created to be like God—truly righteous and holy. EPHESIANS 4:24

You must be holy in everything you do, just as God who chose you is holy. For the Scriptures say, "You must be holy because I am holy." 1 PETER 1:15-16

May you always be filled with the fruit of your salvation—the righteous character produced in your life by Jesus Christ—for this will bring much glory and praise to God. PHILIPPIANS 1:11

But people are counted as righteous, not because of their work, but because of their faith in God who forgives sinners. ROMANS 4:5

Lord, Have Mercy GET ME OUT OF THIS MESS

YOUR "THEN" COULD BE NOW

"*THEN* JESUS WAS LED by the Spirit into the wilderness to be tempted there by the devil" (Matthew 4:1, emphasis mine). That's a provocative verse, is it not? What does "then" mean? *What happened* right before this?

If we go back a couple of verses, we see that Jesus had just been baptized. As he was lifted out of the water, God spoke: "This is my dearly loved Son, who brings me great joy" (Matthew 3:17). Wow. Can you imagine? I'm not sure what happened after you were sprinkled or immersed, but when I came up, all I got were the four verses of "Washed in the Blood of the Lamb" sung by a congregation of eighty who were accompanied by a piano that was slightly out of tune.

After his baptism, Jesus was "in the zone," fulfilling God's will. But then, looking to prove to Satan and the world that his Son was the true Messiah—perfect and sinless in every way—God allowed Jesus to be tempted. Since we're not the Savior of all humanity, God does not tempt us; he already knows the outcome of that test. Between man's frailty and Satan's deception, we have all the opportunity in the world to go sideways.

Sin breaks hearts. Sin is destructive. Sin interrupts our communion with God (sometimes for long periods of time). The whole subject matter is depressing, and honestly, I prefer to prevent the disaster than try to deal with the aftermath.

That's why this chapter is not about sin. It's about temptation. As women, wives, and mothers who are "in the zone" for Christ, we're targets. Our "then" typically happens when everything in our lives is going great and our little families are humming right along. Then, *bam!* Satan slithers in, and we're headed for disaster. *Life. Altering. Disaster.*

If temptation is not something you struggle with, you're probably in greatest need of reading this chapter. Here's the truth: If you don't think you struggle with temptation—or if you can't remember the last time you really had to fight the urge to do something you knew was wrong—rest assured you will be tested soon enough. It's always those of us who don't see it comin'—those who don't realize we are wandering into our own personal wilderness—who get clobbered the hardest and find ourselves on our knees crying out, "Lord, get me out of this mess!"

> I fear that somehow your pure and undivided devotion to Christ will be corrupted, just as Eve was deceived by the cunning ways of the serpent. **2 CORINTHIANS 11:3**

Let's identify our wilderness and find where that serpent lies. We need to remind him who's boss.

KNOW THE COORDINATES OF YOUR WILDERNESS

WHEN JESUS TOOK OFF for the wilderness, he was not naive. He knew he was headed into rough territory. He likely didn't know what was going to be thrown at him, but he knew he would face some extreme conditions. He knew where he was.

I think for many of us, it is not the sin in and of itself that trips us up. We're not idiots; we know right from wrong. Stealing. Slander. Adultery. Idolatry. Denying Christ. Not one of us would say, "Oh, that's a great idea! I want to get involved in *that* sin."

The problem lies in failing to recognize when we are about to enter a place of vulnerability. Our wilderness.

An attribute of mine that Steve found attractive early on was my sense of direction. (Note: not my beauty or my brains; my sense of direction is what turned him on. Good grief!) On an early date, he was impressed with my ability to read a map (without turning it upside down), my intuition (I typically *know* when I'm going the wrong direction), and my ability to return things to their original order (my daddy taught me how to refold the map, which won me major date points). Today, of course, we just type in the address and let our phones or GPS do the thinking for us. You see where I'm going?

We have to be on our toes, alert, and our intuition must be working at all times to determine whether we're heading into dangerous territory. We can't space out, become complacent, or worse—think we're beyond succumbing to a temptation that could destroy our lives and witness. The edge of our wilderness can be deceiving because it is not marked by screeching evil spirits or boogey men. Our journey into our vulnerable state often feels fairly benign and looks something like this:

- My husband and I never talk about anything but the kids.
- As hard as I work, I can't get out of this financial mess.
- I'm overlooked at work; my confidence is stripped.
- I don't feel attractive anymore.
- I'm bored with my life.
- I've lost my sense of self and my identity.
- I'm exhausted from keeping all the plates spinning.
- I try to fit in, but I know I don't.
- I am surrounded by people 24-7, but I'm so lonely.

These are just a few of the desperate places to which our minds wander and that put us at risk for a snakebite; these are the places where we become disoriented and often lose our way.

Temptation comes from our own desires, which entice us and drag us away. JAMES 1:14

Your wilderness is not the same as anyone else's. Figure out your coordinates to know what trouble looks like before trouble finds you.

HANNAH DID IT

OBSERVING CRACKER CRUMBS scattered along the kitchen floor, I asked my precious Ava (who was supposed to be eating her snack at the table), "How did this happen?" Ava looked me straight in the eye and with grave concern leaned in and whispered, "Hannah did it." Well, that's interesting. Ava is an only child, and Hannah lived a few miles away.

Ava, who at the time was not yet three, had made her first major move playing the Blame Game of Temptation and Sin.

Long before this incident, in the early 1970s, the comedian Flip Wilson portrayed a character named Geraldine, who got in trouble with her husband for buying a new dress. Asked how this purchase occurred, Geraldine explained in great detail that the devil *made* her do it. Since this was likely before your time, you may want to look up the clip on YouTube. It's one for the ages as Geraldine takes the Blame Game of Temptation and Sin to a new level.

But Flip's Geraldine wasn't the first to play the game. Adam was actually the originator of this thought-provoking activity. Not only did he blame Eve for his temptation and ultimately his sin, he went a step further by blaming God for sending Eve to him! Wow. Two moves on the game board for you, Adam!

Eve's play was a little more strategic. When asked to answer for her actions, she blamed the serpent for deceiving her. Do we really think Eve was tricked? No way. That girl wanted to be in control and just had to know what God was withholding from her. What a lame blame. But a bonus move for you, Eve; you lied as you blamed!

When we face temptation, we're often tempted to pin our mistakes on someone else, when, of course, we have no one to blame but ourselves. Had we not wandered into our personal wilderness, our desires would not have carried us away. Our temptation has absolutely nothing to do with anyone but us.

Ava blamed Hannah. Geraldine put it all on the devil— she clearly had no choice but to buy that dress. Adam went for the easy out by blaming Eve, but then made the idiotic decision to implicate God. Eve, fueling the argument that "girls are dumb," took the stance that she was just stupid and had been duped. Good one, Eve.

> Remember, when you are being tempted, do not say, "God is tempting me." God is never tempted to do wrong, and he never tempts anyone else. **JAMES 1:13**

Certainly this should give us cause to pause and ask ourselves, *Who's my Hannah?*

THE SMELL OF LUMBER

I WONDER WHETHER SOME SINS are passed on from generation to generation. I don't know if the tendency toward a particular sin is carried in our DNA or if the sin is learned by example, but we can often see a sin pattern repeat itself from parent to child or become a continual stumbling block in ourselves. Sometimes even those desires and interests that aren't wrong in themselves have the potential to trip us up.

Living as serial builders and remodelers is clearly not a sin, but, boy, do Steve and I have a weakness when it comes to home architecture. We are living in our eighth home in twenty-six years. My husband loves the process of designing, building, and fine-tuning a home; I love the outcome. We're codependents. No sooner are we settled in a place than we begin to experience wanderlust. Lord, have mercy if we find ourselves with time on our hands on a Sunday afternoon and we come across an open house for a newly constructed home. The smell of lumber is Steve's "trigger"; it's like an addiction he can barely control.

So what is our plan now that we just finished building our dream home?

1. We know we must avoid places that can feed our temptation. In our case, that means staying away from open houses!

2. Steve knows he can depend on me, and I know I can depend on him. We serve as each other's accountability partners. Surely one of us can "stay strong" and throw away the real estate flyer when it hits our mailbox.

3. We invest our spare time in developing new interests and hobbies. Our wilderness is a lack of other creative outlets, which drives us to explore. Once we're exploring, we're fantasizing. And once we start fantasizing, we pull out the graph paper. Once the sketching starts, we're goners.

4. Steve and I are fully aware of our weakness and know we'll never be completely out of the woods. It's when we let our guard down and casually open the paper to the real estate section that things can go so wrong. We're weak.

Keep watch and pray, so that you will not give in to temptation. For the spirit is willing, but the body is weak.
MARK 14:38

Sweet friend, it is not enough for us to simply know our wilderness. We have to *stay away* from the things or people that Satan will use to draw us in. Sometimes those wilderness thoughts don't make their way into our pretty little heads without help. Stay the heck away.

HEY LUCIFER! COME ON IN!

"GET BACK, SATAN!" If you're reading today's devotion on your smartphone during your quiet time, I think you're safe. But if you're reading this on your phone while your child or husband sits next to you, anxious for your attention, Lucifer has successfully hijacked your time with your family.

Don't get me wrong. Smartphones have absolutely changed our lives for the better. But as with other good things, we often use them for bad. The smartphone, surely the most innovative product of our time, has become the ultimate temptation to distract and disrupt the American family.

A study published in October 2015 by Nottingham Trent University in the UK revealed that the participants, who were between eighteen and thirty-three years old, checked their phones eighty-five times a day and spent a total of five hours a day browsing websites and social sites, as well as using apps. Another interesting fact—this was about twice as much time as the participants said they were using their phones.[9] We're consumed and don't even know it.

While dining out recently, I watched as a family at an adjacent table sat with heads bowed, eyes turned down, and hands in their laps. But they weren't praying. All four were on their phones. Who could possibly have been more important than the other three people sitting in their company? This continued until the server came with their meals.

Everyone seemed dazed when the food arrived. The family sat quietly as they dined. It made my heart hurt.

Contrast this scene with another I witnessed in a restaurant a few weeks later. Four beautifully dressed teenagers walked in, followed by a woman. I made up a story in my head (I love doing this) that the woman was their teacher. I decided they were on some sort of special school outing, probably headed to a symphony or art event. The five of them smiled at one another and conversed casually. Then a man walked in and joined them at the table. *Who's this? Another teacher?* It took me about five minutes to realize the four teens looked like the two adults. Oh, my goodness. This was not a teacher/student exchange—this was a parent/teen exchange!

I was riveted. The kids spoke softly, the parents joined in the conversation, and they all made eye contact! The six of them were so immersed in one another that they didn't know that nosy Mrs. Kravitz (me) was sitting at the next table, eavesdropping. Not once did I see anyone pull out a phone.

Lucifer is sitting at our table. He tempts us with news feeds and updates to avert our attention from the real news—what our kids need to tell us. He is a master at making us and our children feel inadequate—even lonely—as we compare our real lives with the ones portrayed by "friends" on social networks. Lucifer has long been focused on dividing the family, breaking it down, and reducing it to rubble. He used to have to depend on other people, drugs, and crime to do this. Now he just has to put a smartphone in everybody's hand.

If a house is divided against itself, that house will not be able to stand. If Satan has risen up against himself and is divided, he cannot stand, but he is finished!
MARK 3:25-26, NASB

Moms, stand firm and resist the temptation to give in to the draw of anything that will disrupt the lines of communication with your family. Embrace what is great about technology, but refuse to allow it to dictate your family dynamics. Know when you're inviting Lucifer to sit at your table.

WHEN THE JUSTIFICATION DOESN'T HOLD UP

WHEN MARKETING AGENCIES, such as mine, present concepts to a client, we develop what is called a justification. The justification provides the client with the rationale behind our recommendation. It's meant to instill confidence that the concept is sound. Client objectives, factual data on the category, trends in the market, and emotional responses they look to evoke are just a few of the many elements that may be included in the justification. Done correctly, the justification holds up and supports the creative design, and vice versa.

When we begin to take the early steps past temptation toward sin, we may not write a justification, but, sister, it's certainly playing through our heads. The elements usually include these rationalizations: *I deserve*; *I can*; and *I am*.

I deserve to be happy. I deserve to be cherished. I deserve to be rich. I deserve to be noticed. I deserve to be promoted. The justification of "I deserve" is deeply rooted in our over-inflated sense of self-importance.

Here's where this justification falls apart: Every breath we take is a gift from God. Our salvation comes through the grace and gift of his Son. In reality, we deserve nada. Nothing. Zilch. What God deserves is our obedience.

Another element of justification is rooted in control. I can fix this. I can do this. I can hide this. I can protect people. I can protect myself. I can get ahead. I can get around this. When you boil it all down, we think we're better at this game called life than God is.

This justification won't hold up, though, because if we were really in control, we'd never find ourselves in this mess! When we say "I can" and begin to circumvent our situations by resorting to sin, we're pretty well thumbing our noses at God, saying we can control our lives better than he can. What God wants to hear from us is "You can."

Self-righteousness is the element that fuels our "I am." I am good because I rarely sin (and when I do, my sin is not as bad as other people's sin). I am smart. I am attractive. I am needed. I am highly regarded. I am highly valued.

A justification rooted in self-righteousness always falls apart. Only God is the great I AM, and comparing our sin to others' or putting it on a sliding scale of badness doesn't hold up. A humble way of thinking about ourselves and temptation is "I am . . . *not*."

> Don't be fooled by those who try to excuse these sins, for the anger of God will fall on all who disobey him.
> **EPHESIANS 5:6**

You can't minimize your disobedience by maximizing your rationale for heading down that slippery path. Your justification is just not gonna hold up.

CALL THE PLUMBER

I WAS A YOUNG MOM on a budget so tight that it squeaked when the kitchen faucet began to drip like the most sophisticated irrigation system on earth. Thinking through the situation, I realized I could either fix the faucet myself or call a professional and seriously impact the family budget for the rest of the month.

So I decided, *I can fix this. I am able-bodied. I can read. How hard can this be?* Now remember—this was more than twenty-five years before Google and YouTube. HGTV didn't exist yet either. Research, back in those days, meant going to the library, where one would find and borrow a book (or many books)! Let me tell you, it was amazing.

Anyway, let's just say that it was a real Lucy and Ethel moment, only Ethel wasn't there for me to play the blame game with. Within seconds of me attacking the faucet with a wrench, water spewed from it like Old Faithful—a sight to behold. I learned a critical lesson that day: There are some things I am not equipped to fix.

But did I apply that lesson to my faith whenever life came crashing down around my ears, or more important— when my children were in crisis?

No. I have made every conceivable mistake you can think of by trying to fix things for myself or the kids instead of waiting on the Lord and trusting that he had our backs. I've meddled. I've strategized. I've counseled. I've networked.

I've come to the rescue. I've written checks. All because I thought I had a faster fix to the situation than God. Oh, I would not have admitted this to myself—I was too blind to see it. But really—what else would cause me to intervene after I had prayed repeatedly for God's intervention?

Let me tell you, sister, it took me decades to figure out that my "fixing" only interfered with and often delayed the blessing God had in store for my family and me. Not only that, but I finally realized that my attempts at fixing just represented another wilderness I was wandering around in. Not trusting the sovereign will of God is exactly what Satan wants us to do.

Trust in the LORD with all your heart; do not depend on your own understanding. Seek his will in all you do, and he will show you which path to take. **PROVERBS 3:5-6**

When you or your family is in a crisis, you are not likely going to understand the why, if, when, or how of God's solution. But he has one. And trust me, it will be far better than yours. He's the master plumber. Give him a ring.

GOING IT ALONE

HERE'S ANOTHER PROBLEM with temptation: It can isolate us. We're so ashamed that we are or were tempted by a sinful behavior that we can't talk about it. We are left stranded, helpless, and desperate. Or we may minimize the temptation or rationalize our decision to give in to it. We end up prideful, willful, and clueless. Either way, we end up going it alone.

I am Presbyterian (by way of Baptist), but I have always envied the Catholics. As a child, I would sometimes get to attend mass with a friend or family member. In those days we *had* to wear these adorable little doily-lace head covers into the service. My friend, sporting her beautiful prayer beads, drove the point home for me: God wants us to accessorize! Then there was the kneeling, the incense, and the drama of the prayers said in Latin—I was in heaven.

I didn't catch on to the Catholic confessional until I was much older and saw it portrayed on TV. Again I found it most intriguing—especially the wooden-like phone booth where you talk to the priest through a little window. The "sinner"—let's say she's a woman—enters and says, "Bless me, Father, for I have sinned." After a little back-and-forth, the sinner spills her guts. Wow. Just like that—the woman's load begins to lighten. She didn't have to go it alone.

We Protestants don't have to go it alone either. We just need to stop wallowing in our temptations and sinful thoughts or believing that "we've got this." As Christian daughters, we have the most powerful ally and the most capable of counselors. But we need to submit, and that's where we often need help.

While we don't all have a cool little phone booth to enter, we can call on a minister, a counselor, or an accountability partner to serve as our intercessor: someone we can talk with if for any reason we're not quite ready to go directly to God. When we put words to our temptation and say them out loud, it not only makes the temptation real, it gives voice to the internalization of our pain and shame. Healing can begin as our "person" walks us through the perfect three-step plan laid out by the apostle James:

Step 1: *Submit*. Turn yourself over to God.
Step 2: *Resist*. Decide you're not giving in to the temptation.
Step 3: *Celebrate*. Rest assured Satan will cut and run.

Holy buckets! Can facing down Satan and getting our footholds on the slippery slope of temptation really be this easy and this clear? Yep. Says so. Right there in God's holy Word. *But you actually have to do it.*

> Submit yourselves, then, to God. Resist the devil, and he will flee from you. **JAMES 4:7, NIV**

Don't go it alone. Call in the support team. If you don't submit, he can't acquit.

day 45

CAMP COVER-UP

I WAS IN A HURRY as I backed out of my parking place in our office parking lot straight into Steve's car. There was no great damage to either vehicle, so for a split second I considered not "burdening" Steve with the news. However, that would be lying by omission, so I attempted to soften the blow by explaining to him how our bumpers kissed. He was only slightly amused.

A few months later I was distracted as I pulled into a parking place at the grocery store. A terrible scraping noise alerted me that I had pulled in a little too far. Good grief. My confession, stated with the saddest puppy-dog look I could muster, prompted Steve to raise his eyebrows at me as he dialed the auto repair shop.

Several weeks later, while driving in the dark in an unfamiliar area, I drove over a curb while turning a corner. The recently repaired air dam now sported a huge scrape. I couldn't imagine telling Steve *yet again* of my driving foible, but I knew I had best not pick out a bunk at Camp Cover-Up. I came clean.

Just as my accidents were unintentional, so it is with our mistakes. Not even sins—just errors in judgment or good old accidents often tempt us to enter Camp Cover-Up, which sits at the edge of a wilderness of lies.

Hiding shopping bags. Posturing on Instagram. Concealing mistakes the kids have made. Fudging on a customer meeting report. Returning an item that has been used or worn. Failing to admit to an error at work and letting someone else take the fall. Facebooking with *him*. There's a bunk at Camp Cover-Up for every major and minor mistake we make.

Cover-ups are rarely premeditated. Just as I wasn't paying attention when I was backing up, pulling in, or turning the corner—we're not paying attention to the damage we're doing to our own hearts and souls (not to mention to others) when we look to settle into the camp. The bedspreads of deceit, the rugs of hypocrisy, and the curtains of deception make for an uncomfortable cabin to hang out in. It's a terrible place to stay.

> Be on your guard, not asleep like the others. Stay alert and be clearheaded. 1 THESSALONIANS 5:6

Heads up, sister. Steer clear of Camp Cover-Up. The wilderness of lies is one you sometimes can't escape.

OUR EXITS ARE NOT ALWAYS CLEARLY MARKED

IMAGINE YOU'RE ONE of more than eighteen thousand fans standing and swaying with the crowd as your favorite band performs onstage. This concert is sold out, and the music and performances are amazing.

Though you're enjoying the show too much to think about it, at the back of your mind you know what you'd do if a fire broke out: You'd likely make a beeline for the door. It would be clear that (a) you were in danger and (b) you needed to get out. But if there was just a little smoke, you might conclude that the haze was simply the result of the band's fog machine. You wouldn't panic or run for the nearest exit. You would continue to rock out, even though that small voice in your head might say, *Something's not quite right, but why move toward the exit and risk missing the rest of the show?*

What if you were wrong? What if there was a fire, but now it was too late to get away?

Most of the time, when we get closer to yielding to temptation, we're having a pretty good time. I remember a pastor saying once, "If you're not having fun sinning, you haven't found the right sin." While we're rocking out to some fun temptation, a fire is actually smoldering beneath our personal stage. As things heat up, we have to begin looking for our exits.

God always provides us a way out of the wilderness; he provides us an exit to the temptation to prevent us and those we love from being consumed by sin. But our exits are not always clearly marked. Sometimes we have to look for them. I've found mine often are marked with:

An opportunity. God often brings something new and fresh to distract me from my temptation.

An emergency. There's nothing like a crisis to snap me out of my wayward thinking.

Scripture. I can't read the Word of God and not see my exit clearly marked.

Sermons. More than once while sitting in church I've asked myself, *How in the world did* that *sermon get planned for today?* God uses pastors to mark my exits.

Family. I need only one family member to notice something is up. "What's wrong?" "What are you thinking about?" "Are you okay?" "Did I do something wrong?" These are God's flashing neon signs: *Run this way.*

The temptations in your life are no different from what others experience. And God is faithful. He will not allow the temptation to be more than you can stand. When you are tempted, he will show you a way out so that you can endure. **1 CORINTHIANS 10:13**

It's our job to *look* for the exits God has given us. And then we need to run for them. It's not just smoke. It's fire.

WHAT'S BENEATH
THE SURFACE

THERE'S NOTHING LIKE a cool dip in the pool—especially on a hundred-degree day in Texas! The water sparkles like a disco ball under our hot Texas sun, and the crystal clear water all but beckons me to come on in. I love swimming. What I don't love is swimming with things that I can't see. There's some ugly stuff below the waterline.

Stuff like makeup and suntan lotion. Hair gels and sprays (we still use lots of spray in Texas). Perfume and soap. And of course, anyone who has hung out in a pool with little kids knows that what they leave behind can be even nastier!

When we swim in a polluted pool, we're only somewhat aware of what's in the water. We lull ourselves into a false sense of security, as the chemicals mask the danger. But as we paddle around, we don't have to accidentally swallow the water to absorb what's swimming in there with us. A little warm water and our pores open right up, and we suck in the yuck without even knowing it.

Unfortunately, we don't always need to put on our swimsuits to dip our toes into filthy water. Every day we swim in polluted pools that are disguised as normal, inviting, and even healthy everyday events. Contaminated pools are actually located everywhere we turn.

The filth of sexual promiscuity and sexual exploitation is rampant in our pools of entertainment. The beautiful people in movies and music, as well as the female entertainers whose performances sexualize women and girls, have taken us back thirty years. I'm embarrassed that we don't see the crap floating in our pool and demand that it be cleaned up. How would we do that? By no longer supporting them with our entertainment dollars. By not buying that magazine. By not going to her concert. By not buying from that fashion house or retailer.

Another dirty pool, often located in our own neighborhoods or workplaces, is the one "everyone else is swimming in." Lies and deception. Excess. Envy. Anger. Pride. Sexual infidelity. Unethical business arrangements. Tax evasion. Crude and vulgar language. Self-idolatry. We barely even notice all these tiny contaminants floating around us. They're all beneath the waterline, and we're just paddling around, soaking them up. Or adding to the filth.

So how do we avoid the pollution in our own communities? By valuing integrity above personal comfort. By making the right choice rather than the easy one. By standing firm for what is right, what is good, and what is honoring to God.

> Don't do as the wicked do, and don't follow the path of evildoers. Don't even think about it; don't go that way. Turn away and keep moving. **PROVERBS 4:14-15**

The temptation to go along and swim around in this filthy mess is our own personal and spiritual challenge. We don't let our kids go twenty-four hours without a bath, but we're all swimming in a cesspool. Lord, help us see what's beneath the surface and look for a cleaner pool.

CHILD, PUT SOME CLOTHES ON

I PULLED AVA FROM THE TUB and cuddled her up in a big fluffy towel to dry her sweet, soft body. All of two and a half, she wiggled out of my arms and streaked across the house in her bare nakeds.

I, of course, took off running after her (which resulted in great squeals of delight from her). My job was to catch her and cover that precious little tushie. As I gathered her up in my arms, I said, "Child! Put some clothes on!" Which yielded more wiggles and giggles.

Our God runs after us, too. Don't think for a second that he turns his back on us when we lose our battle and yield to temptation and sin. Oh no. He comes looking for us in order to cover our shame. After Adam and Eve ate of the tree of the knowledge of good and evil, they hid from God. Their nakedness, now a symbol of the physical and emotional shame they felt as a result of their sin, sent them scrambling for cover and sewing coordinated outfits of fig leaves. They were stripped bare and exposed to their very souls.

I think some of the sweetest words recorded in the Bible are those of God asking Adam, "Where are you?" (Genesis 3:9). How incredible that the Creator of the universe would run after us, *especially* after a fall from his grace. Just take that in for a second. Rather than ignore us or punish us with his silence or absence, God comes looking for us to wrap us in his big fluffy towel of forgiveness and unconditional love. Even then we sometimes run the other way, allowing our guilt and embarrassment to put miles between us and the God we adore. He's desperate to catch us and hold on to us for dear life—but we sprint away.

Whenever we find ourselves in a place of temptation or sin, one of the most important things we can remember is the Lord's unfailing forgiveness and provision. We might experience shame as the result of our sin being found out. We might suffer the serious consequences of our actions. We might even separate ourselves from God as we run away from him. But he doesn't separate himself from us. Just the opposite—he chases us down in our nakedness.

The LORD God made for Adam and for his wife garments of skins and clothed them. **GENESIS 3:21, ESV**

Child, stop running.

day 19

PLAN FOR THE WORST; HOPE FOR THE BEST

I'M A PLANNER. My family gives me grief for my "overplanning" of our extended family vacations, but I can't help myself. I want to be prepared. And let's just say this plainly: I don't care how much you love your family, family vacations can be stressful.

This is how I plan: After some research and discussion, we finalize our destination, and I begin to build a fabulous (and I mean fabulous) color-coded Excel spreadsheet. Flight numbers, hotel locations, and confirmation numbers are included along with sightseeing destinations (by day and time) and associated ticket confirmation numbers and addresses. I even specify free time and free days (when each family member can pull away from the pack). Breakfast, lunch, and dinner options are outlined, along with reservation details in the event that we don't come across a better meal option. There's nothing worse than traveling with five adults and one child when more than half of them are suffering from low blood sugar. Did I mention this is a *fabulous* spreadsheet? Yes, I'm a geek.

Excel is my way to plan for the worst and hope for the best. We might not need 50 percent of the details I include on our itinerary, but they are there if we need them. And trust me, we have needed these details more times than we haven't.

Just as we strategize for a great vacation, we must prepare ourselves for lives of success. To do that, we must have a plan to avoid the day we might succumb to a temptation that would ruin our Christian walk; decimate our mental, physical, and emotional health; completely dismantle our families; and *grieve* God. To spare ourselves from that heartache, we must create either a mental or physical spreadsheet that defines:

1. *Our destination.* What does a successful life look like for us today and forty years from now?
2. *Our transportation.* What are the vehicles (churches, friends, and organizations) we can use to get there?
3. *Our planned activities.* What pursuits are we investing in to get us closer to this fabulous destination?
4. *Our free time.* How can we spend our unstructured time in a way that benefits our destination?
5. *Our meals.* What are we reading and taking in to feed our hearts and minds on our journey?
6. *Our confirmation numbers.* What Scriptures do we have at the ready?

Prepare your minds for action and exercise self-control. Put all your hope in the gracious salvation that will come to you when Jesus Christ is revealed to the world. **1 PETER 1:13**

A well-planned journey will help keep us away from dangerous areas. What is your plan to avoid that wilderness? Plan for the worst, and put your hope in the best—God himself.

THE WILDERNESS OF SUCCESS

PTA PRESIDENT. Director of marketing. Fund-raiser chairperson. Bank vice president. Top salesperson. CEO.

These titles sound great, right? They mean our hard work has paid off and we've reached a level of success we once only dreamed about. But success can lead us into a wilderness all its own. The very nature of our achievements and what it took to get us there can cause us to slip into this wilderness, undetected. Regardless of our roles—work, mothering, or volunteering—we're in danger.

Moms, hear me out on this. This is important for you and for your very successful kids (whether varsity cheerleaders or first-string football players; first-chair orchestra members or stars of the school play; valedictorians or National Merit Scholars) as they edge the line of this wilderness.

When we enjoy a string of wins—let's call them short-term successes—we gain a superhuman sense of confidence. We think, *I know what I'm doing.* Those who've had several short-term successes over a long period of time often develop a superiority complex. In the business world, professionals with winning records are called "subject matter experts"; in other areas, they're considered superstars. Subject matter experts or superstars often enjoy a great degree of influence. They can shape ideas; write rules and regulations; or build or dismantle organizations. Those who keep their pride in check are the ones who build successful people, enterprises, and societies. But those whose egos take control end up as a sad equation:

$$Overconfidence + Superiority + Undue\ Influence =$$
$$A\ Know\text{-}It\text{-}All\ Headed\ for\ a\ Fall$$

It is incredibly difficult for highly successful individuals to keep their bearings and not fail someone or something. Too often success fuels overconfidence, which can lead to a wilderness of flawed judgment, impatience, and disrespect; a place where outwardly successful people begin to discount others because they think their ideas are more important and valuable than anyone else's. Without keeping their pride in check, it's just a matter of time before these individuals hit the floor hard.

I know this wilderness personally. I most often find myself at the edge when I feel our company work product has been challenged. Pride sometimes causes me to lose my footing—and nothing good has ever come from that.

Pride goes before destruction, and haughtiness before a fall. **PROVERBS 16:18**

Experience, wins, and insight are what propel us toward positions of influence. Humility, kindness, and inclusion will keep us there—and out of the wilderness.

GET ME A HOE

ONE DAY WHEN I WAS FIVE, my three-year-old cousin, Dana, and I were playing in the garage at his home across the street from mine. We were big buddies. Our game that morning was leaping over a step leading onto his back porch, hopping back and forth like a couple of wigged-out kangaroos.

After jumping back and forth for a few minutes, I looked down, and there, snugged up against the step riser, stretched out for all the world to see, was a twelve-foot-long water moccasin. Well, it probably wasn't twelve feet long, but when you're five, everything appears greater than it is.

Our caretakers were two African American women whom we loved as our second mothers. Savannah (whom we called Vannah) watched over my cousins, and Lerlene (whom we referred to as Lene) had cared for me for as long as I could remember. They were strict. They were kind. And, oh, were they entertaining!

I called out, "Vannah, come look at this snake!" Well, you cannot image the reaction and the size of her eyes as she yelled—and I mean yelled—"Lord, have mercy! Ellen, run and call Lerlene. And get me a hoe."

Such great excitement ensued (nothing much ever happened in a small town of seven hundred, especially on a weekday, so my cousin and I were beside ourselves as the drama unfolded)! Lene ran toward the garage (this in itself was entertaining) with the hoe in hand.

As we all stood and stared at the oh-so-very-still snake (did I mention it must have been twelve feet long?), Vannah laid out the plan: While we were fetching the hoe, she had put a pot of water on the stove to boil. She would throw the water on the snake, then Lene would chop its head off with the hoe. Dana and I were not asked for our thoughts on this plan, but we quietly concurred (because of our extensive experience killing snakes).

We were instructed to stand back (good call) as Vannah threw the boiling water on the snake. It writhed and curled like you wouldn't believe, then Lene came in for the final kill with the hoe and *whack!* Off came its head.

A perfect plan. Perfectly executed. That, my friend, is how you kill a snake.

> "Get out of here, Satan," Jesus told him. "For the Scriptures say, 'You must worship the LORD your God and serve only him.'" Then the devil went away, and angels came and took care of Jesus. **MATTHEW 4:10-11**

When you see Satan in the wilderness, don't mess around. Put some water on to boil, call a friend, and get out your hoe. That serpent will writhe away, the angels will come, and Jesus will take care of you. I've seen it work.

IF YOU ONLY REMEMBER THIS

IF YOU GIRLS WOULD HAVE ASKED ME if I ever, *in a million years*, would have written extensively on the topic of temptation, I would have called you cray-cray. Not because I don't have personal experience with the topic, but because I do. And there lies the rub.

Being a grandmother, you'd think I would have aged out of this by now, but I find that's not true. My professional success, my loving marriage, my sweet kids, my being a Christian author—none of these things has shielded me from Satan's tricks. He knows my weaknesses, and he's out for me, just like he's out for you. So if you don't remember anything else from this chapter, remember this:

Stay vigilant.

This is not the time to be distracted. Yes. I wrote that with a straight face. By the very fact that you're a mom, I know you are distracted . . . by everything! But you can't be too busy with "stuff" to recognize when you're stumbling into your wilderness. Stay vigilant.

This is not the time to be careless. When life is humming along, you can't take for granted that you're in the clear. You're not. Lucifer's got us in his sights and knows exactly how to manipulate us. Being reckless about what or who you think about or how you react to success or failure can be the very thing that leads you to destruction. Stay vigilant.

This is not the time to be ignorant, indifferent, or negligent. Your life, your marriage, and your family are at stake. Watch carefully so you can detect danger. Don't for a second think you can turn your eyes away. *Watch* for the signs of temptation. Stay vigilant.

When Ava is with me and proposes to do something that is daring and could lead to injury, my standard line is: "No, ma'am. Not on Sugar's watch." When that child is with me, I am alert. Ever awake. I am not oblivious to the dangers and disasters that could befall her. I am on my game.

> Stay alert! Watch out for your great enemy, the devil. He prowls around like a roaring lion, looking for someone to devour. 1 PETER 5:8

I pray you will be on your game too.

I SAID THIS PRAYER *for You* LAST NIGHT

Father God, I come before you knowing if ever there was a time to pray boldly, it is now. Cover my sister, Father. Show my new friend the coordinates of her wilderness; help her to identify where she is vulnerable, and give her clarity and courage to find her way out of danger.

Strengthen her conviction to refuse Lucifer's entrance into her home. Fortify her to stand firm against Satan so he cannot penetrate her mind or the psyches of her kids. Prepare and equip her with insight, forethought, and self-control. Show her when she's swimming in a polluted pool, and give her the courage to get herself and her family out.

Humble her determination to fight this temptation on her own. Give her the maturity to stop justifying her temptation and to own her failings. Show her how to rely wholly and only on you.

Guide her to a new, higher place—one where she can see and discern clearly the tricks Satan has used on her before. Provide her a higher understanding of the nature and destructive power of temptation.

Keep her eyes open. Keep her mind alert. Keep her heart attuned to you for your glorification.

Keep her vigilant.

I pray this with great expectation, Lord, that you will steel up this mom with the resolution to firmly say, "Get back, Satan." In the name of Jesus Christ, our Rescuer, our Savior, who died for our sins, I boldly and humbly pray. Amen.

HIKING GEAR

I'M NOT MUCH OF A HIKER. I'm more of a Ritz-Carlton Spa girl. But I've been on a couple of hikes with our good friends Barbara and Tom. They live in Breckenridge, Colorado, on a mountain that is ten thousand feet above sea level. I kid you not, I need an oxygen mask just to walk up their driveway! But when in Rome (or in Colorado) . . .

Steve and I once showed up for a Sunday morning hike at the base of a trail near their home. I was outfitted in what I considered appropriate hiking attire for August in Colorado: a T-shirt, a pair of Lululemon yoga pants, and my favorite Nikes. It seemed like a reasonable wardrobe choice until we began scaling the rock face of a mountain like a herd of goats. As two *very* elderly Japanese couples scampered up ahead of us with their walking sticks, khakis, hiking boots, and hats, I felt, well, a bit underdressed and ill-prepared.

I don't want you ill-equipped as you wander onto the trails of temptation. I want you fully prepared. If one of these verses speaks to your heart, that's the Holy Spirit. He's whispering, *You might need this one day.* So here it is, God's holy Word for your hike up the mountain. Godspeed.

Then Jesus was led by the Spirit into the wilderness to be tempted there by the devil. **MATTHEW 4:1, EMPHASIS MINE**

And a voice from heaven said, "This is my dearly loved Son, who brings me great joy." **MATTHEW 3:17**

I fear that somehow your pure and undivided devotion to Christ will be corrupted, just as Eve was deceived by the cunning ways of the serpent. **2 CORINTHIANS 11:3**

Temptation comes from our own desires, which entice us and drag us away. **JAMES 1:14**

Remember, when you are being tempted, do not say, "God is tempting me." God is never tempted to do wrong, and he never tempts anyone else. **JAMES 1:13**

Keep watch and pray, so that you will not give in to temptation. For the spirit is willing, but the body is weak. **MARK 14:38**

If a house is divided against itself, that house will not be able to stand. If Satan has risen up against himself and is divided, he cannot stand, but he is finished! **MARK 3:25-26, NASB**

Don't be fooled by those who try to excuse these sins, for the anger of God will fall on all who disobey him. **EPHESIANS 5:6**

Trust in the LORD with all your heart; do not depend on your own understanding. Seek his will in all you do, and he will show you which path to take. **PROVERBS 3:5-6**

Submit yourselves, then, to God. Resist the devil, and he will flee from you. **JAMES 4:7, NIV**

Be on your guard, not asleep like the others. Stay alert and be clearheaded. **1 THESSALONIANS 5:6**

The temptations in your life are no different from what others experience. And God is faithful. He will not allow the temptation to be more than you can stand. When you are tempted, he will show you a way out so that you can endure.
1 CORINTHIANS 10:13

Don't do as the wicked do, and don't follow the path of evildoers. Don't even think about it; don't go that way. Turn away and keep moving. **PROVERBS 4:14-15**

Get Me Out of This Mess

Then the LORD God called to the man, "Where are you?"
GENESIS 3:9

The LORD God made for Adam and for his wife garments of
skins and clothed them. **GENESIS 3:21, ESV**

Prepare your minds for action and exercise self-control. Put
all your hope in the gracious salvation that will come to you
when Jesus Christ is revealed to the world. **1 PETER 1:13**

Pride goes before destruction, and haughtiness before a fall.
PROVERBS 16:18

"Get out of here, Satan," Jesus told him. "For the Scriptures
say, 'You must worship the LORD your God and serve only
him.'" Then the devil went away, and angels came and took
care of Jesus. **MATTHEW 4:10-11**

Stay alert! Watch out for your great enemy, the devil. He prowls
around like a roaring lion, looking for someone to devour.
1 PETER 5:8

Lord, Have Mercy   HELP ME BE GOOD

THE FORCES OF GOOD AND EVIL

THE WAR BETWEEN GOOD AND EVIL that rages within us is summed up, quite clearly, in Romans 7:

> I don't really understand myself, for I want to do what is right, but I don't do it. Instead, I do what I hate. **VERSE 15**

Oh, Lord, have mercy. This is me in a nutshell! You, too? I set out to do good, but something in me goes wrong. Instead of being kind and gentle, I find myself being rude, impatient, and headstrong. These are attitudes I hate, yet I still behave in these ways! What's wrong with me?

> I want to do what is right, but I can't. **VERSE 18**

Yes! Thank you, Paul the apostle, for putting it so clearly. I really want to be a good person, but I can't. I want to be that woman who has filled her belly with the fruit of the Spirit— you know the ones: love, joy, peace, patience, kindness, goodness, faithfulness, gentleness, and self-control. I want to be like that. But for the life of me, I can't keep it together!

> I want to do what is good, but I don't. I don't want to do what is wrong, but I do it anyway. **VERSE 19**

Why is it so hard for me to do what is good? I don't understand it. I promise myself before I leave the house that

I'm gonna be good and kind and patient with everyone I meet, but then, almost without warning, all my fruit goes bad. Stinky bad.

> But if I do what I don't want to do, I am not really the one doing wrong; it is sin living in me that does it. **VERSE 20**

Say what? It's not really me, but the evil in me that is winning? Well. No wonder I have such a hard time being good. I've been set up by an evil force!

> The sinful nature wants to do evil, which is just the opposite of what the Spirit wants. And the Spirit gives us desires that are the opposite of what the sinful nature desires. These two forces are constantly fighting each other, so you are not free to carry out your good intentions. **GALATIANS 5:17**

Well, this is just great. Not only am I prone to wander into a wilderness, I have an evil force that drives me there! Where can I get help?

> Let the Holy Spirit guide your lives. Then you won't be doing what your sinful nature craves. **GALATIANS 5:16**

Lord, have mercy! Is it really this easy? Yes, my friend, it is. Good can win this fight and will win when we're willing to rely on him for help. We all try from time to time to go it alone, but unfortunately we know what that gets us—and it's not good. Let's try a new tactic by calling on our Helper (the Holy Spirit) for help.

LOVE YOUR NEIGHBOR (& THAT PRISSY LINDSEY AT PTA)

LOVING YOUR NEIGHBOR, when the person isn't lovely, is one of the hardest tests of being a Christian. It's like a pop quiz God just drops on us every now and then. I've yet to ace it consistently.

But I love people. I really do. I love people who are thoughtful, kind, and considerate. I love people who are nonjudgmental, openhearted, and just. I love people who love me (and I love them a lot when they love me first). I love my family, friends, coworkers, neighbors, and Christian sisters who see things and do things my way. Oh. Now we're getting somewhere. Maybe this is why I fail the quiz with such regularity.

When Scott returned to us after having been missing for three and a half years, he became stable in his sobriety. You'd think everything would be hunky-dory—but it wasn't. Scott had his own plan for his life and his relationships, and these were not aligned with our plans for him. Loving your slightly batty neighbor or the sickeningly sweet PTA president is one thing; demonstrating unconditional love when your child is at odds with your family and values is like trying to ace a trigonometry test handed to you in the middle of PE.

As the battle of the wills continued over the next year,

Scott continued to surge forward on the field while I lost yardage. I dug in, principled, on what we could or could not allow as Scott ran further and further from us, culminating in our—get this—estrangement. This was not lost on our granddaughter, Ava, then four.

As we drove down the street one Saturday morning, out of the blue she said, "Sugar, I miss Uncle Scott." I looked up in the rearview mirror and replied, "Yes, I do too."

"Sugar, when is he coming to have dinner with the family?" I squirmed. "Honey, I'm not sure."

Ava, eyes locked on mine, said with a very corrective tone, "Sugar, he's family." A four-year-old just graded my test, and I flunked.

Ava didn't have a clue what all had gone on between us, nor did she care. Her love, pure and inclusive, demonstrated that it didn't matter who was right or wrong. She only knew that love is unconditional, but all parties must be present to win.

So how did Scott, Steve, and I bridge the canyon that existed between us? We agreed to disagree.

We all have more in common than what divides us. That's true of our family, true of our fussy next-door neighbor, and true of that prissy Lindsey at PTA.

Owe nothing to anyone—except for your obligation to love one another. If you love your neighbor, you will fulfill the requirements of God's law. **ROMANS 13:8**

You've been warned: A pop quiz is coming your way. And I hope a four-year-old is not grading yours.

SHAME ON ME

ABOUT SEVENTEEN YEARS AGO, Steve and I shared with our Bible study class that Scott was a drug addict. We were embarrassed that our parenting had failed and that our son had become a member of the underworld of drugs, but we desperately needed their prayers.

We were uncomfortable. We were in distress. We were ashamed. And we were humbled in a way that I can't even find words to describe. We never would have known such deep trust in God, reliance on his will, and grace extended to us by our fellow brothers and sisters without this adversity.

The humiliation we parents feel over our kids' actions, however, is another ball game. It is embarrassment on steroids:

A son who went too far. Rape.
A daughter who touched her student inappropriately.
   Sexual assault of a child.
A son whose drug habit spun out of control. Theft.
A daughter who tried to get ahead. Embezzlement.
A son whose hatred and mental illness consumed him.
   Mass murder.

This is real life. I know moms whose kids fit three of the five profiles above. They are devout, devoted Christian moms who faced public and private humiliation.

In the aftermath of their children's mistakes, they were lost to despair. Their children's sin resulted in shame and disgrace for their families. But these women all survived. Their ability to put their trust in God and his will and to humble themselves to receive grace from God and their Christian sisters carried them through.

> The reward for trusting him will be the salvation of your souls. **1 PETER 1:9**

The reason I wrote this entry is twofold: If you're not the one crying out for grace, you will be the one called to extend it. Your child might or might not be the sinner. You might or might not be shamed. But prepare your soul now in the event that one day, if you're so called, you can extend love and grace to a sister who needs it.

In her book *A Mother's Reckoning: Living in the Aftermath of Tragedy*, Sue Klebold, mother of Columbine shooter Dylan Klebold, writes, "If God sends us love on earth, I truly believe it is delivered through the actions of people. During that terrible time, we were sustained by the care of those around us."[10]

> Most important of all, continue to show deep love for each other, for love covers a multitude of sins. **1 PETER 4:8**

There but for the grace of God go I. Shame on us if we don't show up in someone else's shame.

day 56

CONTROL YOURSELF

Over my professional career, which now spans thirty years, I have come to the conclusion that if people have six key attributes, they will likely achieve a significant level of professional success. Only in the past few years have I come to realize that without two of these six key attributes, many people will fail to achieve personal success. The list? Drumroll, please:

1. Self-control
2. Integrity
3. Adaptability
4. Aptitude
5. Passion
6. Humility

I could write a book (and hope to one day) on these critical personality traits and how they relate to our witness and our careers. All are God given, and all can be honed. However, besides integrity, none is more important than self-control. For you see, without it, the others are rendered impotent in our professional and personal lives.

Successful men and women who understand that self-control is literally self-preservation and protection ultimately live lives of greatness to the sweet end. They will finish this race strong, because they've adopted a mind-set of self-regulation.

Mom, you're a fabulous witness to your friends and family when you:

Spend less. Nothing says self-regulation more than putting money in a savings account.

Read more. Those who have self-control want more of it. Internal discipline is honed through research and learning.

Are reliable. Moms with self-discipline can be counted on to follow through; they will never leave you hanging at the concession stand filling popcorn bags alone.

Gossip less. Moms with self-control have more important things to do, like building a life of greatness for themselves and their families.

Are on time. Most self-controlled people are also respectful of others.

Whisper more, yell less. Self-regulation means quieting the mind and taming the emotions long enough to get the whole story before going off the deep end. Our words and our tone are a fabulous example to our little ones.

A person without self-control is like a city with broken-down walls. **PROVERBS 25:28**

Moms who exercise self-control teach their children by example. Way to set them up for success!

YOUR WORST DAY EVER

"This has been the worst day of my life!" Eight-year-old Ava was completely and suddenly distraught as she stood in the doorway crying, dripping wet from her shower. Shauna, shocked by the abrupt outburst, couldn't imagine what Ava had been holding back all evening. She loved second grade at the Episcopalian school she attended. Still, Shauna knew that Ava had recently been on a little bully-ette's "hit list," so she prepared herself for the worst. She dried Ava off, cuddled up close, and asked for details.

"First off, in chapel this morning as I kneeled for prayer, my hands slipped and I bumped my head on the prayer rail. It was really loud and everyone could hear. I'm sure I have a bruise."

"No," Shauna consoled her, "no bruise, and I bet others were praying, rather than laughing at you." (Hope springs eternal.)

Knowing there must be more to the story, Shauna urged her on, "What else?"

"Well," she answered, "While I was washing my face in the shower just now, I got soap in my eyes."

Shauna patted her back and said, "Oh. I'm sorry. I'm sure that was painful, but I think you're going to be okay. What else?"

Ava blinked. Nothing else. And with that, the child got up and went about her evening.

According to the National Institutes of Health, our DNA contains four chemical bases with scientific-sounding names and abbreviations: adenine (A), guanine (G), cytosine (C), and thymine (T).[11] But I think the NIH has overlooked a fifth chemical base present in many women: drama queen (DQ).

Don't believe me? Ask a first-grade girl and boy the same question, "How did this happen?" Then just watch and listen. The little girl will gesture with two or more appendages because she can't utter a word without them. She will raise her voice several decibels, and her pupils will dilate to the size of frying pans as she relates the story in excruciating detail. When you ask the little boy what happened, he will blink, shrug, and mutter, "I dunno."

Many of us were born with significant levels of drama queen in our system. (And Ava's got DQ *bad*.)

How we react to the worst day ever—or even an inconvenience—is telling when it comes to our faith. We can hardly expect others to follow our example and understand what it means to follow Christ if we operate in a state of panic, distress, fear, anxiety, or defeat at the slightest bump of the head or after a few suds in our eyes. Should you or your husband lose your job, should your sixth grader be suspended from school, or should you get rear-ended at the drugstore, your faith will be on display.

I've seen this play out in our business. As challenges arise, mistakes are made, and client strategies shift, Steve and I must be flexible and calm. Christ's provision, plan, and solutions are always more abundant, more timely, and more creative than anything we could come up with on our own. Our experience has taught us to operate in a state of peace when we're having our "worst day ever" and to let that peace be a witness to our faith.

"I know the plans I have for you," says the LORD. "They are plans for good and not for disaster, to give you a future and a hope." JEREMIAH 29:11

For all of us DQs, it's important to remember that those in our orbit feed off our energy. Let's make sure it's peace and hope and not Armageddon we're serving at the breakfast table.

ARE YOU *KIDDING* ME?

ON DECEMBER 26, 2015, a tornado tore a four-mile path through the eastern Dallas suburbs of Garland and Rowlett. Hundreds of homes were destroyed, and thousands of people were displaced. In addition, eleven lives were tragically lost.

On December 28, 2015, the storm raged on, creating havoc for Christmas travelers. Of the 2,800 flights canceled that day, more than 1,300 were at Chicago's O'Hare airport, resulting in a sea of grumpy faces scattered along the terminal walkways.

Each story was covered extensively by the world news on the morning of December 29.

At the scene in Rowlett, a young father was featured as he held his two-year-old son, surveying the damage; his home was pretty well gone. He calmly told the reporter that his young wife had passed away the previous year, but that he and his son were fine and they would be okay. He expressed gratitude, hope, and confidence as he patted and swayed with his toddler, who was hoisted high on his shoulder.

The news anchor then broke away from that young father to report on the chaos at O'Hare. Looking straight into the camera, a young woman—all of maybe thirty years old—yelled a string of obscenities at the reporter for a good thirty seconds straight. It seems her canceled flight had ruined her life forever. I was floored as I listened to her rant. I don't even know that many curse words!

Never have I seen such a contrast in perspective in under four minutes.

Maybe I hadn't had time to fully process the young father's loss of wife and home—I was so sad. But as the crazy blonde ranted and raved over the disservice done by the airline, airport, and weather, all I could think was, *Are you kidding me?*

And then I wondered, *How many times am I that woman?* How many times do I overreact to things that have minimal consequence and are pretty much outside of anyone's control? How often does my self-righteous indignation get the best of me?

> Be thankful in all circumstances, for this is God's will for you who belong to Christ Jesus. **1 THESSALONIANS 5:18**

But perhaps the better question is *Would I be like that man?* If my world were to crumble, would my witness remain strong? Could I lean into God's will and be thankful for his provision for each day? Would I exercise hope above hysteria? Gratitude above grief? Confidence above concern? Would I freak out or faith out? It's worth thinking about, now, before the storm hits.

YOUR GLUTES AND GENEROSITY

"You're not firing your glutes," my trainer told me as I stood on one leg with my head down, barbells in each hand and looking toward the floor. She went on to explain that I was expending a lot of energy for little payoff by failing to concentrate on this vital muscle group. Good to know.

Our time and witness are often wasted, too, when we fail to exercise generosity well. I have several great role models in my life, both women and men, who are openhanded.

Only months after we first met, my friend Barbara dropped off a beautiful drawstring bag filled with jewelry she had recently expelled from her collection. Handing me the bag, she said, "This is for Ava." Barbara remembered my telling her how Ava and I loved playing dress up and brought something to share with her.

On our next playdate, Ava, almost three at the time, sat on the floor awaiting the surprise from "Ms. Barbara," whom she'd not met. As Ava pulled out beautiful rings, glistening beads, and bracelets, her eyes widened, and with a hushed but serious tone she told me, "Sugar, this is *good* stuff."

Yes. This is good stuff.

Barbara only gives the good stuff—not just when it comes to chokers and bangles either. Barbara knows how to give the good stuff of hospitality, generously opening her home to overnight guests for days or weeks at a time.

She and her husband, Tom, give money, energy, and time to underprivileged families. Their generosity goes beyond "check the box" to "change a life." And equally important, Barbara generously and enthusiastically cheers her friends on. She celebrates them. She never withholds a compliment. She's never too busy. She's never emotionally "unavailable" to listen. She brings the good stuff to her friendships.

You know you're practicing true generosity when it requires some sacrifice—so don't think for a second that selfless giving is without focus and intention, or in any way easy. To the receiver the gift looks effortless, but when it's done right, it is a workout.

> Generous people *plan* to do what is generous, and they stand firm in their generosity. ISAIAH 32:8, EMPHASIS MINE

Like our glutes, our generosity needs to be fired up and exercised with purpose and *on purpose*. We need to give the good stuff or we're just wasting time.

PRAY THIS, NOT THAT

IF YOU'RE A CHRISTIAN MOM (and I assume you probably are since you've made it this far through the book), you already know this: There will always be someone who is not going to like you. And that *someone* will often be your kids—and their friends—and their friends' parents.

Let me encourage you to begin praying now that God will bless your impact, even if—okay, when—you're the least popular person on the face of the planet.

Mom, you're different. I'd like to tell you that you fit in, but you don't. You weren't called to be a part of this world and its nuttiness; you were hand-selected by God to be a woman of impact. A change agent. A person of influence, prominence, and significance. A woman with this type of calling is likely to go against someone's grain (and that someone is probably fourteen or fifteen years old).

When my kids were young, parents were parents. We taught our children to respect authority and to follow rules. Once Steve and I heard of someone hosting a party where the parents allowed the teenagers to drink, but that was an anomaly. As parents, we understood and embraced our role. But things are changing.

I heard evidence of that last week on a news program. In the "old days," when our children were growing up, we taught them to call adults by their first names with a Mrs. or Mr. preceding it. I was Mrs. Ellen to all of our children's friends except those whom we counted more among "family." Today, the news report noted, many children are encouraged to call their friends' parents by their given names because "we want our children to feel they are equal." News flash: They're not our peers. They are children.

Our witness relies on our ability to positively impact and influence the lives of our kids and their friends. We can't do that if we're considered "one of them." How much wisdom and insight is your thirteen-year-old expelling? See my point?

> You are not like that, for you are a chosen people. You are royal priests, a holy nation, God's very own possession. As a result, you can show others the goodness of God, for he called you out of the darkness into his wonderful light. 1 PETER 2:9

We are not our children's peers. We are not that cool. We are women of significance—the ones these children will remember for wisdom, love, and courage. Our children will not remember us for being popular; they will remember us for being different. Rejoice.

RUNNING LOW ON FRUIT

I AM ALWAYS KIND to the ladies at the dry cleaner (even when they accidentally stretch out my pants). I express faithfulness, peace, and self-control with our clients. I strive to show joy and goodness to our employees. I pour love out to our kids, and I am patient with Ava. So which fruit of the Spirit is missing? And *who* is missing?

Gentleness. And Steve. Oh, I'm so ashamed to share this story with you, but here goes.

During the nine-month construction phase of building the house we live in today, we had three major floods. When it wasn't raining, we were waiting for the water to dry up so our contractors could get back to work. A one-week delay stretched into three weeks; three weeks stretched into months. We watched the days tick by on the calendar, knowing we had sold our current home and were scheduled to move June 4, ready or not. It was "not."

How incomplete was it? For about four weeks, Jesús—the man in charge of installing our tile—and his team were in the bathroom with me as I put on my makeup and fixed my hair for work. It was *that* incomplete.

For three months, Steve worked remotely to oversee the construction and its completion. After weeks of one major setback after the next, I was convinced that this was the way our life would be forever. Nothing in the house was finished. Nothing was working.

And I turned into a total witch.

Our then twenty-five-year marriage, which was as sweet as a marriage can possibly be, became depressingly tense. Poor Steve. As he battled contractors and delays by day, he had to battle with me by night! This went on for weeks before the Holy Spirit really convicted me: My impatience and desire for ease and comfort were trumping the very thing my husband needed most from me at the moment—gentleness.

Months later, as I write this entry, I sit in my office in our beautiful new home. I am thrilled to say that our life and wonderful marriage have returned to normal (*especially since I put away my broom*).

> The Holy Spirit produces this kind of fruit in our lives: love, joy, peace, patience, kindness, goodness, faithfulness, gentleness, and self-control. **GALATIANS 5:22-23**

Don't let your fruit run low, especially the fruit of gentleness. Your husband may be starving for it.

THAT FISH SMELLS

STEVE AND I ARE FRIENDS with a very successful business-man who is a devout believer. One evening many years ago, we were chatting with him about the challenges and joys of owning our own businesses. As the conversation turned to our experiences in dealing with others who proved less than honorable, he said, "If I see a fish emblem on the tailgate of a pickup, I know that's someone I probably don't want to do business with." Unfortunately our friend had been on the receiving end of more than one breached contract by business owners who drove vehicles sporting this fine adornment.

The fish emblem he was referring to is the one often used by folks who identify as Christians. Like men and women might wear a cross to represent their faith, this is Christian jewelry for a pickup truck. The design originates from the Greek word *ichthys*, which means "fish." Early believers created an acrostic of the Greek letters to spell out *Iesous Christos Theou Yios Soter* or "Jesus Christ, Son of God, Savior."[12]

Well. You see why this might be a problem. When we expose ourselves as Christians, as we're called to do, and then blow it by lying, gossiping, operating dishonestly, being rude, and acting unfairly, those *sins of the spirit* cause our fish to stink. And everyone can smell it. Our outward expression and inner spirit must be aligned when we wear the brand of Christ, especially when we work for or serve with others.

Whether we're employed by a business, sitting on a committee, or serving as a volunteer, our witness is on display for both believers and nonbelievers alike. I will tell you this: Both groups expect more from believers than from our non-believing counterparts. We're more critically judged when we err. We are held to a higher standard, and when we fail, we evoke a greater amount of disdain compared to nonbelievers. If that isn't enough, it often takes much longer to repair the damage to our reputations. Not fair, you say?

> For everyone to whom much is given, from him much will be required. **LUKE 12:48, NKJV**

Given the gift of our eternal salvation, upholding our end of the witness bargain seems the least we can do.

On the flip side of this story, a landscaping company we do business with is owned by a very strong Christian. There's no Christian jewelry on his truck. He goes the extra mile to serve us. He speaks kindly to his laborers. His pricing is fair and his work is always finished beautifully and on time. What's more is he never signs off a text, e-mail, or voice message without saying, "Have a blessed day."

His fish don't stink.

> Work with enthusiasm, as though you were working for the Lord rather than for people. **EPHESIANS 6:7**

We can't let our fish get smelly either.

IT'S REALLY DARK IN HERE

I WALKED CLOSELY BEHIND AVA as we entered the Lebanon Silver Mine near Georgetown, Colorado. Sporting our yellow hard hats, we looked oh so official and most capable. But as Ava followed the narrow walkway farther and farther into the mine, she turned back to me with a worried brow and whispered, "Sugar, it's really dark in here."

"Yes, it is," I replied, wanting to add, "but it's darker out there."

Data collected in May 2015 by Gallup revealed that 72 percent of those polled believed the state of moral values in the United States was "getting worse." This did not come as a surprise to me but what did get my attention was that 22 percent thought we were "getting better."[13] Hmm . . . I wonder what TV channels they're watching that I'm not.

Last Thursday evening as I cooked dinner, a selfie of Kim Kardashian flashed across the television screen. Mind you, this was at 6:30, when thousands of children across America were also tuned in. What was so shocking that I dropped my ladle? She was completely nude—except for a few body parts that the "news program" had blackened out.

Sisters, it's gotten dark out there.

When a pornographic photo is considered newsworthy and appropriate for audiences of all ages, we know we had better get out our flashlights.

Which is why you and your witness to the love of Christ is more important than ever.

The light shines in the darkness, and the darkness has not overcome it. JOHN 1:5, NIV

Wouldn't you love to stir up an uprising of mothers across this country to cry in outrage over the deteriorating state of our media? Please tell me who cares what Kim does? Give me one reason why her selfie is newsworthy. Wouldn't you love nothing more than to organize a virtual march, emoticon-fist pumping in the air, to challenge Beyoncé, JLo, Miley, Katy, and the like to return to promoting their incredible God-given talent instead of their sexuality? At the same time, we would applaud entertainers such as Alicia Keys, Adele, and Sara Bareilles who are the embodiment of powerful, confident women. These ladies have achieved great success while fully clothed. It saddens me to see that we have been taken back thirty years, returning us to caricatures of attention-starved sex symbols. Imagine if all of our female entertainers just said, "No. We're better than that."

But I'm not a rabble-rouser, and you're really busy with math homework. Still, there *is* something we can do: We can *all* turn on our lights.

In the same way, let your good deeds shine out for all to see, so that everyone will praise your heavenly Father. MATTHEW 5:16

This little light of mine, I'm gonna let it shine. Our collective light is brighter than the darkest of dark. Sister, let's turn it on.

GUILTY AS CHARGED

A HEADLINE FOR A MAGAZINE ARTICLE caught my attention: "I Am Silently Judging You."

I knew it! I've seen it in people's eyes as they hold back their negative thoughts.

I once thought this was an affliction of only the upwardly mobile and those born into old-money families. When I was just starting out as a young parent and my social circle was limited to other women at church and the parents of my children's friends, I never thought much about it. We were all so busy trying to raise kids and make ends meet that we didn't have time to measure or critique others. Not once during my early to late twenties do I remember judging my sisters, and only once did I realize I was being judged. Get this: The woman whom I had looked to as an older, wiser role model in my Sunday school class was serving as a self-appointed undercover fashion police. Ugh. Witness busted.

As I moved up the socioeconomic ladder, however, I knew I was being sized up on everything from my family lineage, education, neighborhood, house, and car to my weight, fitness level, fashion sense, and the condition of my collagen.

In intellectual and academic circles, women are judged by their IQs, publications, alma maters, number of degrees, high-profile speaking engagements, and awards.

In mommy groups, judgment swirls around the topics of working (whether inside or outside the home), breastfeeding, permissiveness, styles of discipline, the choice of private or public schools, the loss of (or addition to) baby weight, and the number of lattes you need to get through the day.

In the business marketplace, women are judged as to whether they are too harsh or too soft, too outspoken or too quiet, too friendly or too aloof, too ambitious or too comfortable, and whether they spend too much time at the office or not enough.

Even women in Bible studies are silently judged by their attendance and the degree to which they have completed their homework assignments.

Have you been judged? Yes, you have. Like me, have you sat in silent judgment of others? I'm not surprised. Here's one for us *all* to commit to memory:

> You will be treated as you treat others. The standard you use in judging is the standard by which you will be judged.
> MATTHEW 7:2

Ohh . . . I'm not thinking one more bad thing about someone's hair!

PLEASE BE GOOD

THE LAST THING I WOULD SAY to my kids before dropping them off for a playdate was "I love you." It was always preceded by "Please be good." Do you say that too?

Let's consider what *being good* sounds like to a six-year-old on a playdate:

You have to share. Whatever you're playing with, you don't get to hog it.

You have to let others choose. As the guest, you might be invited to choose what you play or you might get to go first in a game, but if not, you just have to suck it up.

Do not pout. If something doesn't go your way, don't pull that Patty Pouty routine.

Do not argue. You have to be agreeable to work out problems (even if you're right).

Be polite. Say please and thank you. And say it like you mean it!

Eat whatever you're served. No wincing or making gagging noises.

We want our children to be good. And when they're not good, we want them to at least fake it. Why do we want our little angels not to act like the little hooligans they are at home?

First, we want them to be invited back. Let's be honest, having two hours of peace and quiet on a Saturday afternoon is heavenly! We want them to put on a good face for the hope of a return invitation. Mama needs some downtime!

Second, their behavior, whether good or bad, is a direct reflection of the way we've raised them—or at least to a great degree it is. You can attempt to direct some children until you're blue in the face, and they won't "get it." But it still reflects back on us when our children are lovely. And when they're not.

So it is with us. When Christ says "be good," we need to remember that our actions reflect directly onto him. He's provided us great direction in his Word; sometimes we get it, but sometimes we don't.

Do we share or hog?
Do we humbly follow or insist on our way?
Do we sulk when we should just move on?
Do we swallow our pride to be more agreeable?
Do we allow others to go first (in line, in traffic, etc.)
     even when we're in a hurry?
Do we express our gratitude with deep sincerity?
Do we gratefully accept what we've received without
     wincing?

I am fully convinced, my dear brothers and sisters, that you are full of goodness. You know these things so well you can teach each other all about them. **ROMANS 15:14**

When we can't *be* good, sisters, we're still called to *act* good. Let's not allow our poor behavior to reflect poorly on him.

PASS THE SALT AND THE PEEPER, PLEASE

OUR CHRISTIAN WITNESS is in peril every time we open our mouths. It doesn't take much for it to tank.

A flippant response to a girlfriend. A curt reply to a husband. An agitated directive to a child. A dismissive tone with the waiter, a coworker, or the checker at the grocery store. And boom: We sound like everyone else in the world.

Our everyday encounters count. The strength of our commitment to Christ is reflected in the sound waves between our vocal cords and another's ear. His love, his mercy, and our salvation are on display every time we open our mouths. The responsibility is frightening, especially when we know we often blow it with our own family before we pull the Eggos from the toaster.

> May the words of my mouth and the meditation of my heart be pleasing to you, O LORD, my rock and my redeemer. **PSALM 19:14**

I have been known to blow it. I have said things to those I love that run counter to the character of the God I profess. As I've aged, my self-control of the wagging tongue has slightly improved, but it's still an everyday struggle and one that is often top of mind. However, there's another element of this opportunity to testify to his love that we often forget: the power of eye contact—the window to our soul.

When I speak to others and my witness is at stake (hello—when is it not?), I look them in the peepers. My tone, my word choice, and my meaning are communicated very differently from when I'm not looking at them—both as I send my thoughts and as they're received. Just try it for yourself. It's a total game changer.

When Steve and I dine out, whether it is at one of the "besties" we patronize often or at a onetime dining event, we try to make eye contact with everyone who serves us. We've noticed how surprised and engaged our water servers become when, as they refill our glasses, we look up at them, into their eyes, and say thank you. When we purposefully live the spirit of Titus 3:2—"Be gentle and show true humility to everyone"—we are rewarded too. We know we've made a connection with a few of God's children—whether they are believers or not. And when I'm wearing my cross, I can't help but wonder if they make the connection, either consciously or subconsciously, to the love of the one who hung there for our salvation.

Everyone who has eyes will be able to see the truth, and everyone who has ears will be able to hear it. ISAIAH 32:3

When you and I open our pretty little mouths, we are more responsible than the average bear for what comes out. Season your words to everyone and spice them up with a little "peeper." Everything will taste and sound so much better.

DON'T OVERTHINK IT

SO WHAT DO YOU SAY to skeptics who question your beliefs? You know. The ones who challenge your faith, put you on the spot, and make you feel like an idiot?

Of all the definitions of *apologetics* I have read, one of my favorites is: "Apologetics is the discipline of defending a position (often religious) through the systematic use of information." I like this definition—which shows up in a number of books and online articles—because it doesn't use the word *argumentative* (Merriam-Webster) or describe it as a branch of theology (dictionary.com).

When I am challenged to defend my faith, I can honestly say that I pretty well fail to make my case through the "systematic use of information." My lack of theological training—the understanding of historical time lines, lineages, Greek, Hebrew, and everything else that's woven in the Good Book—leaves me vulnerable and ill-prepared. And, of course, these conversations never go down with a person of average intelligence. Oh, no. The one on the other side of the "debate" is always a real smarty-pants. So in addition to feeling vulnerable and ill-prepared, I feel stupid.

What I've come to understand was that until I amass enough knowledge to defend my truth (we're not off the hook—every one of us has to learn how to do this), all I really need to do in the moment is not overthink it.

Gabby Douglas, the US gymnast who brought home

three Olympic gold medals, doesn't shy away from discussing her faith. Just before heading to Rio for the 2016 summer games, Gabby told a reporter why her training playlist features Christian music: "I love sharing my story and I love sharing about my faith. God has given me this amazing God-given talent, so I'm going to go out and glorify His name."[14] After reading that quote, I had to glance back at the URL at the top of my screen to see if I hadn't landed on *Christianity Today*'s web page. But, no, it was *Cosmopolitan* magazine's online site. With authority and conviction, Gabby just put it out there. And they published it!

Unlike Gabby Douglas, Annabel Beam was unexpectedly thrust into the spotlight. At the age of nine, she fell headfirst thirty feet into a hollowed-out tree that she'd been climbing. Miraculously, when rescuers reached her, they discovered she'd suffered no serious injuries. Even more striking, she appeared to have been cured of a chronic intestinal illness following the accident. It was during the five hours that she was inside the tree that Annabel says she went to heaven. Her story became the movie *Miracles from Heaven* (starring Jennifer Garner as Annabel's mother).

When Annabel responds to skeptics who don't believe she went to heaven, she calmly and sweetly says that she has no doubt Jesus spoke to her there. She's not bothered when people don't understand. Annabel is so confident in her knowledge that she doesn't need to argue her point. She knows what she knows, and she doesn't need to convince anyone else. Her sweet tone and deep conviction say it all.[15]

You will know the truth, and the truth will set you free.
JOHN 8:32

But since we don't do backflips and it's not likely we'll have a movie made about us, how do you and I defend our position as believers? A transformed life lived for Christ will say more than words ever can. Until we master apologetics, we shouldn't overthink it. Just say it. Just live it. He will take care of the rest.

SUPERTHRIVE YOUR LEGACY

I CAME TO KNOW Mrs. Claudine O'Neal over lunch one day as my new friend Carla introduced me to her mammaw, posthumously. Carla was reading the chapter "What Mammaw Said" from my first book and recognized the two old girls had a lot in common. (FYI—if you're not from the south, Mammaw is a name often given to grandmothers. It's why I have Ava call me Sugar.)

Like my grandmother, Mammaw Claudine was a force to be reckoned with. She was confident, convicted, and clear as she rightfully laid claim to her matriarchal position: "I am the root of this family." (Mammaw Claudine lived in Tuscaloosa, Alabama, so it's not pronounced "root," it's pronounced "RU-it," requiring a long breath and approximately one and a half syllables, if you can imagine.) Before we were halfway through our salads, Carla and I agreed that we were blessed beyond measure because our grandmothers' roots ran deep.

I know more about roots than I should. Especially tree roots. When they are healthy and run deep, a tree can withstand adverse weather conditions, strong winds, and even a transplant or two. When they're shallow or frail, the roots fail to carry the nutrients needed to the branches and leaves. Long term, a tree with shallow roots will slowly die.

Last week, almost a year to the day since we transplanted a couple of very large trees, Steve and I noticed that they were beginning to look sickly. An arborist suggested we try the root-stimulating product SUPERthrive. I kid you not—that's the name. When you pour this stuff on the roots of a newly transplanted tree, the lifesaving nutrients cause the tree to take off. A quote from the late founder of the company, Dr. John A. A. Thompson, can be found on the home page of his company's website: "My whole idea is to try to leave the world better off for wherever I touch it."[16] Well, Dr. Thompson, shouldn't we all—especially when it comes to our families? We need a bit of SUPERthrive for our legacy so that the roots we lay down today will sustain future generations through lots of changes and storms.

I know. Right now you just want to get through your first grader's level 5 reader or off the junior high graduation planning committee, but believe it or not, there's a good chance someday you're going to be a proud, doting grandmother to one or more. So now is the time to SUPERthrive your legacy by:

> *Gaining confidence in your God.* Make note today of the prayers he answers and the ways he's redeemed your life. The stories will be told for generations to come— over lunch.
>
> *Staying convicted of your principles.* Your moral authority is being transferred today and will be passed by your grandbabies to their babies. (Can you imagine the world they'll be living in?)
>
> *Being clear as a Christmas bell.* Speak the truth in love, but speak it. You are the *root* of this family. Claim it.

Blessed are those who trust in the LORD and have made the LORD their hope and confidence. They are like trees planted along a riverbank, with roots that reach deep into the water. Such trees are not bothered by the heat or worried by long months of drought. Their leaves stay green, and they never stop producing fruit.
JEREMIAH 17:7-8

There will be no root rot on our watch because we're producing good fruit with confidence, conviction, and clarity. Those little branches of yours are already reaching out, and one day it will be their children who remember you fondly and say, "I was blessed beyond measure." Yes, now is the time to pour on that SUPERthrive.

PULLED TOGETHER

Since I was going to be on TV, I wanted to look my best. The producers insisted I not wear black or white. What are the predominant colors in my wardrobe? Black and white. Though I did not have much time to prepare or shop, I was fortunate to find a fabulous hot pink dress trimmed with gold grommets at the hem just in time. I accessorized it with a long gold-and-white necklace, small gold dangly earrings, and a pair of black high-top Converse tennis shoes. My outfit was totally pulled together.

Not really. Oh, the description—cameras, lights, dress, and jewelry—is true right up until the mention of the Converse tennis shoes. What would that have done to my chic look? Honestly, it would have completely destroyed it.

Our witness to the love and peace of Christ is not much different. Like the most beautiful ensemble ever, we're eye-catching. When we're rocking the fruit of the Spirit, we look different from the rest of the world because our jewelry box and drawer of accessories is full of stunning pieces. When we wear a gentle spirit during a crisis or challenge, others can *see* our peace. When we adorn our lips with thoughtful, kind responses to everyone, we sound different. As we embellish our outfit with strands of patience for all—from those we love to total strangers—our look is completely pulled together. And as we open our lovely little handbag and give compassionately and passionately, it will be our big beautiful heart, not the brand of the purse, they will remember.

But let one gossipy, hateful string of words or profanity roll off those pretty pouty lips, and our outfit is completely ruined. Our beauty as daughters of the King isn't just blemished. In the eyes of the world, we look like a runway disaster.

You and I sit in a strange place as messengers of his love. We have a great responsibility that we can't ignore. Every "accessory" we add to our outfit, good or bad, has consequences.

> Since God chose you to be the holy people he loves,
> you must clothe yourselves with tenderhearted
> mercy, kindness, humility, gentleness, and patience. ·
> **COLOSSIANS 3:12**

We must choose our look carefully. Especially since he chose us to be *his models* walking on the runway of the world.

IF YOU ONLY REMEMBER THIS

NOT LONG AFTER THE IDEA for a slumber party surfaced, the girls in my sixth-grade class began planning the details—and it sounded like it was going to be a great time. Unfortunately, my parents had already promised another family that the three of us would have dinner with them that night, so I was unable to attend. Little did I know that my absence at the soiree would make me a living, breathing target. It was my only personal experience with bullying. *Distraught* is not a strong enough word to convey my emotional state as a sixth grader. Fortunately, the abuse lasted only a short time, but as I grappled with how to deal with my mean-girl classmates who had previously been my friends, I went to my mammaw. Because she was always wise and direct, I knew I could count on her counsel.

As I poured out my heart, I told her what I wanted to say to them. She shook her head and said the words all of us have heard at some point in our lives: "If you can't say something nice, Ellen, don't say anything at all."

If nothing else sticks with you from this section, I hope this one word will: *edify*.

I know now that Mammaw was telling me to edify. *Edify* is not a word we commonly use, but few words in the English language convey as much as this one does as it relates to the quality or *process* of our witness. To edify is to "instruct or benefit [someone], especially morally or spiritually."[17] It is to enlighten. It is to uplift. It is to improve.

The opposite is obvious: to tear down, demoralize, weaken, make worse.

To edify, we must think carefully before we speak, sometimes even choosing *not* to speak. To edify, we must consciously turn on our witness filter—a spiritual filter that removes contaminants, strains the good from the bad, and blocks certain thoughts and actions, while allowing others— that are positive—to come through.

Unfortunately, our witness filter is easily clogged. When it's pride in the filter, we feel the need to defend ourselves. When hurt gets stuck in there, we believe striking back with words will alleviate our pain. And when fear is trapped in the filter, we strike out in protection mode. None of these edify.

So write this word on your heart or stick it on your fridge. Let it be a reminder that our witness is to benefit. It is to uplift. And it is to improve. Anything less is unacceptable.

> Do not let any unwholesome talk come out of your mouths, but only what is helpful for building others up according to their needs, that it may benefit those who listen. And do not grieve the Holy Spirit of God, with whom you were sealed for the day of redemption. Get rid of all bitterness, rage and anger, brawling and slander, along with every form of malice. **EPHESIANS 4:29-31, NIV**

Back to the story: The mean girls apologized. All was forgiven. And thanks to Mammaw's words, I didn't blow my witness (at least not *that* time).

I SAID THIS PRAYER *for You* LAST NIGHT

Father, I am humbled to enter your presence and for the privilege to commune with you and to know personally your love for me and my friend.

I thank you, Lord, for this precious soul and the light she shines for you. I pray that her witness will be powerful and that others will be drawn to that light and come to know you better. Place those who need to be loved on her heart and mind—especially when they're difficult to love. Give her a yearning and a capacity to demonstrate your unconditional love in a way that is fresh and new.

Bless her with a discerning spirit, one that is slow to judge and quick to seek forgiveness. Empower her witness and elevate her in new ways in the eyes of her children so that they will see what a good and holy and godly woman their mom is.

Bless her with sustainable peace and a godly perspective when life goes off the rails and with tenderhearted mercy when her friends are shamed. Fortify her walls of self-control, focus her actions so she can impact others, and provide her a generous heart to always and only give the good stuff.

Enable this woman to provide a gentle touch to the person, likely her husband, who needs it most. Help her to deliver the fruit of the Spirit in every interaction: with her children, her husband, her parents and in-laws, and the stranger on the street. Remove all pride, pain, and fear from her heart that she might uplift, enlighten, and improve those in her midst.

Bless her witness, Father. Protect it. In the name of your Son, Christ Jesus, I pray these things. Amen.

PRETTY IS AS PRETTY DOES

LAST WEEK, STEVE AND I packed up our SUV and headed south to Austin for a few days. I enjoy road trips over air travel because I get to take everything with me—from my pillow to full-size bottles of shampoo and conditioner to my blow-dryer. For this trip, I'd packed every conceivable lotion and potion in my suitcase to ensure I looked my best.

But when we rolled back into Dallas, you wouldn't have believed I had even packed a hairbrush. My hair was stringy from being blown in the wind. My mascara was all but gone from having laughed so hard (I tear up good with a hearty laugh). And my clothes were a rumpled mess from wiggling around in my seat for three hours. So much for looking my best. Unless looking my best means looking like his best.

No product on earth can add to or detract from our beauty as can our witness for Christ. So I will fret less about what I pack in my suitcase and more about what I pack in my heart. I hope you will do the same so that everyone you meet will say, "What a beautiful woman she is."

I don't really understand myself, for I want to do what is right, but I don't do it. Instead, I do what I hate. . . . I want to do what is right, but I can't. I want to do what is good, but I don't. I don't want to do what is wrong, but I do it anyway. But if I do what I don't want to do, I am not really the one doing wrong; it is sin living in me that does it. **ROMANS 7:15, 18-20**

The sinful nature wants to do evil, which is just the opposite of what the Spirit wants. And the Spirit gives us desires that are the opposite of what the sinful nature desires. These two forces are constantly fighting each other, so you are not free to carry out your good intentions. **GALATIANS 5:17**

Let the Holy Spirit guide your lives. Then you won't be doing what your sinful nature craves. **GALATIANS 5:16**

Owe nothing to anyone—except for your obligation to love one another. If you love your neighbor, you will fulfill the requirements of God's law. **ROMANS 13:8**

The reward for trusting him will be the salvation of your souls. **1 PETER 1:9**

Most important of all, continue to show deep love for each other, for love covers a multitude of sins. **1 PETER 4:8**

A person without self-control is like a city with broken-down walls. **PROVERBS 25:28**

"I know the plans I have for you," says the LORD. "They are plans for good and not for disaster, to give you a future and a hope." **JEREMIAH 29:11**

Be thankful in all circumstances, for this is God's will for you who belong to Christ Jesus. **1 THESSALONIANS 5:18**

Generous people *plan* to do what is generous, and they stand firm in their generosity. **ISAIAH 32:8, EMPHASIS MINE**

You are not like that, for you are a chosen people. You are royal priests, a holy nation, God's very own possession. As a result, you can show others the goodness of God, for he called you out of the darkness into his wonderful light. **1 PETER 2:9**

The Holy Spirit produces this kind of fruit in our lives: love, joy, peace, patience, kindness, goodness, faithfulness, gentleness, and self-control. **GALATIANS 5:22-23**

Help Me Be Good

For everyone to whom much is given, from him much will be required. **LUKE 12:48, NKJV**

Work with enthusiasm, as though you were working for the Lord rather than for people. **EPHESIANS 6:7**

The light shines in the darkness, and the darkness has not overcome it. **JOHN 1:5, NIV**

In the same way, let your good deeds shine out for all to see, so that everyone will praise your heavenly Father.
MATTHEW 5:16

You will be treated as you treat others. The standard you use in judging is the standard by which you will be judged.
MATTHEW 7:2

I am fully convinced, my dear brothers and sisters, that you are full of goodness. You know these things so well you can teach each other all about them. **ROMANS 15:14**

May the words of my mouth and the meditation of my heart be pleasing to you, O LORD, my rock and my redeemer.
PSALM 19:14

Everyone who has eyes will be able to see the truth, and everyone who has ears will be able to hear it. **ISAIAH 32:3**

You will know the truth, and the truth will set you free.
JOHN 8:32

Blessed are those who trust in the LORD and have made the LORD their hope and confidence. They are like trees planted along a riverbank, with roots that reach deep into the water. Such trees are not bothered by the heat or worried by long months of drought. Their leaves stay green, and they never stop producing fruit. **JEREMIAH 17:7-8**

Since God chose you to be the holy people he loves, you must clothe yourselves with tenderhearted mercy, kindness, humility, gentleness, and patience. **COLOSSIANS 3:12**

Do not let any unwholesome talk come out of your mouths, but only what is helpful for building others up according to their needs, that it may benefit those who listen. And do not grieve the Holy Spirit of God, with whom you were sealed for the day of redemption. Get rid of all bitterness, rage and anger, brawling and slander, along with every form of malice. **EPHESIANS 4:29-31, NIV**

Help Me Be Good

Lord, Have Mercy AS I RAISE THESE KIDS

PERFECTION

SHE'S PERFECT! This was my first thought as I looked into the eyes of my pink, five-pound newborn. (I may have said these words too, but I was a bit delirious after twenty-four hours of "natural" childbirth. *What an idiot.*) Oh, yes. I was more than naive on multiple fronts.

My dear friend and ob-gyn, Dr. Kathryn Waldrep, once told me, "The greatest desire for all expectant mothers and fathers is to have a perfect child. But those of us who have raised a family know there's no such thing. We're all flawed."

Kathryn went on to say, "Advanced medical technologies enable screenings and tests that today can reveal in utero a child's imperfection weeks before their birth. I no longer begin the difficult conversation with 'I'm sorry . . . ,' but instead am able to tell parents, 'You're ahead of the game. You already know your child's imperfection. All children have them. Sometimes we just don't know what they are for a while.'"

What profound truth. From the womb to the tomb, we're all flawed. Oh, the baby might look perfectly perfect, but it's a total illusion. She's not. You just haven't found out her "issue."

Some moms get a glimpse of their children's imperfections around the age of two. That's when I realized Shauna wasn't exactly "spotless." She toddled into the kitchen one Wednesday morning with one goal for the day: to give me a run for my money. And she did. Weighing in at just under twenty-five pounds, she had the goods on me and was intent on making my morning existence as miserable as possible. Later that day, completely frazzled, I asked a much older, wiser woman in my life, "What's wrong with her?" She didn't even try to soften the blow as she burst out laughing, "Oh! You just realized she's not perfect! That's funny!"

Funny? No. This concept had never crossed my mind. Sadly, some moms are lulled into a false sense of security and fail to experience the reality of their child's issues until he or she goes off the deep end at thirty. Not only is the epiphany delayed (and rude—you'd think you were out of the woods by then!), the fallout from the imperfection is often devastating; a thirty-year-old creating havoc in the world can do a lot more damage to himself or herself and others than a two-year-old can sitting on your kitchen floor.

Raising flawed children, when we're flawed ourselves, supports my theory that it is an absolute miracle that this institution we call a family continues to survive. But our modern Christian family is alive—and while not perfect, it is well—by the grace of God.

God arms me with strength, and he makes my way perfect.
PSALM 18:32

(Especially when my kids aren't.)

PREPARE FOR BATTLE

THERE ARE SOME THINGS we must go to battle over. I've decided macaroni and cheese is not one of them.

Is there anything more frustrating than getting your child to eat a balanced diet? How in the world can a two-year-old exercise such complete and utter control during the family dining hour?

Shauna, our first, would eat anything I set in front of her. Spinach. Tomatoes. Chicken. Beef. It didn't matter. If I fixed it, blended it, and spooned it—she ate it. By the time she was three, her food pyramid was rocking.

Then Scott came on the scene (adopted at four months), and when I started him on baby food, the child wouldn't eat anything that wasn't sweet. I fretted, I forced (of course you know how well that worked!), and I bribed. Mealtime was a nightmare.

And it didn't get any better for about twelve years. There would be many a tear shed over eating a green bean or tasting the sweet potato. One bite, and lots of gagging ensued. Try as I might, he wouldn't back down. What a waste of good ammunition.

What I saw as defiance was simply very sensitive taste buds. As he aged, Scott grew out of it. Today when we dine out, Scott is the one at our table most likely to order rabbit or squid. I look at him and just shake my head, saying,

"Who are you? Do you know how many wasted hours I spent in battle with you over food?"

Ava is a bit like Scott. Last week she told me she would eat some broccoli only if I covered it with cheese until she couldn't see the green part. Cheese pizza. Grilled cheese. Cheese quesadilla. There's a theme. But she's not dragging me onto the battle stage. This one, I already know, is not worth fighting.

What are those battles we should take on?

Anything and everything that threatens our child's self-worth. Anything and everything that threatens our family's ability to communicate, trust, and grow together. Any person, organization, or concept that is counter to our personal and our family's walk with Christ. When we see these threats, we must arm ourselves well and commit the battle to him.

Put on every piece of God's armor so you will be able to resist the enemy in the time of evil. Then after the battle you will still be standing firm. **EPHESIANS 6:13**

Save your energy for the real fight against the enemy, and forfeit the fight over macaroni and cheese. You're not gonna win that battle anyway.

NOT WHAT I ORDERED

THE WAITER PLACED THE plate of eggplant parmesan before
me. I looked at the dish, then up at him, and blinked. He
asked, "Did you not order the eggplant parm?"

"No, I ordered veal parmesan."

The waiter apologized and offered to replace the meal,
but I told him the eggplant would be lovely. (Dinner without meat? Hmm . . .)

Sometimes we don't get the dinner we ordered. Sometimes
we don't get the kid we ordered either.

Even though we accept that our kid won't be perfect, we
still have a vision for him or her. From the time that baby
is snug in the womb, we create an idealized version of what
he or she will be like. The class president. An All-State base-
ball pitcher. A little ballerina performing in *The Nutcracker*.
A STEM student who scores his first patent as a sophomore.

But instead we get eggplant.

Scott was about three when I suspected that one day he
would tell me he was gay. Thinking in those days (1983)
that I might be able to reroute his course, I did everything
I could to guide him toward "boyish" activities, one of
which was soccer. After his first soccer practice, he declared
emphatically, "This is not a nice game. People try to take the
ball away from you." Nope. The Olympics would not be in
his future. What I got instead of a heterosexual athlete was
probably the sweetest child that has ever walked the face of

the earth. Scott's drug addiction was something else I didn't request, but his challenges brought me eye to eye with the grace of God more than any single event of my life. He's not what I ordered because I couldn't have known the blessing of him, just the way he is.

Shauna was seven when she got into the car after her dance lesson and proclaimed her disdain for tap. I did everything I could to encourage—okay, bribe—her to stay in dance, but softball had captured her heart. My dream of her taking the stage at Radio City Music Hall was dashed. She would not be a Rockette. What I got instead was a competitive, hardworking, hilarious kid who delights me to this day. When placing my order for a little girl, I didn't know to request an "old soul" who is wise beyond her years. I am blessed beyond measure to have her just the way God made her.

I am absolutely certain we are blessed with the children we're supposed to have, rather than the ones we have idealized. God knows exactly what he's doing with his matchmaking.

Here am I, and the children the LORD has given me. We are signs and symbols in Israel from the LORD Almighty, who dwells on Mount Zion. ISAIAH 8:18, NIV

I didn't get what I ordered. I got something better. Oh, and as for dinner—the eggplant parm is my new favorite.

EMULSIFY

SOME KIDS AND PARENTS in blended families are about as compatible as 90 percent humidity and a good hair day. You can tease, pull, spray, and pray, but things still go flat.

Steve had never been married when he took on a wife and two kids. Our adjustment period was simplified (ha—I bet he would disagree!) by the fact that he did not have children. All Shauna, Scott, and I had to do was "break him in"! Poor fella. He was like a deer in the headlights for about three years.

For those of you who are working (and Lord, have mercy—it's work!) to blend your families, I lift you to our heavenly Father and give you this word of exhortation: emulsify. No, it's not a biblical term; it's a cooking term.

I am sorry to say that for years my salad dressings were just not that tasty. I bet I tried twenty-five recipes, and regardless of the ingredients, they always left me disappointed. After some research, I learned what I was doing wrong: I needed to emulsify! If you have a blended family, you might want to pick up the technique too.

To emulsify, you mix together ingredients that will not naturally blend—like Dijon mustard, diced shallots, honey, olive oil, and vinegar—and whisk away. But here's the trick to making a great salad dressing: While whisking, you must add the olive oil one drop at a time. Yep! A drop! Then whisk. Then another drop and whisk. Then another and another. Then a very slow trickle. Whisk a bit longer and—voilà!—a beautiful dressing.

To blend your families, do the same. Slow down to drop kindness on those who are irritable. Drop selflessness on those who are threatened and lash out. Drop empathy on those who are sad and confused. Drop compliments on those who try but sometimes fail. Drop prayers of thanksgiving on their ears so they know they are treasured. Drop patience on yourself and your husband when the easiest of things becomes a struggle. And then add a slow, steady stream of a good sense of humor because nothing will make a family gel like a hearty laugh.

> May God, who gives this patience and encouragement, help you live in complete harmony with each other, as is fitting for followers of Christ Jesus. **ROMANS 15:5**

If you find yourself a Carol Brady, without an Alice, a hunky husband, and six adorable kids who get along famously, well, sister, I'm so sorry—life isn't a sitcom. And there's your drop of reality for the day. It's harder than it looks in TV Land. I'm praying for you.

day 15

THE SILENT KILLER

THERE IS A SILENT, ODORLESS, DEADLY POISON in our homes, and it's not carbon monoxide.

It is the result of a wrongdoing, a hurtful word, maybe even a terrible sin. The pain vaporizes into bitterness that builds up. Sometimes a window is opened and a breeze draws through, allowing the fumes to dissipate for a while. But then they're back.

The poison taints everything and everyone in the house. Parents don't think it affects their kids, but they're pretty sensitive to the toxin. They may not know what it is, but they know that something bad is in the air. Instead of headaches, this contamination induces shame. Instead of sleepiness, it chokes out love, intimacy, and affection. The person controlling the valve will say they're "working through it," and they likely are. But for how long and after how many months of breathing this contagion, can the family survive?

The inability to forgive and extend grace is like killing your family and yourself with a caustic chemical. People who have been hurt might think they have every right to their deadly gas. I say they're wrong. They're dead wrong.

If we cannot deny our pride and refute our ego to extend grace, forgive, and move on, how can we, as sinners for whom Christ died on the cross, expect forgiveness ourselves? Wallowing in bitterness and embracing resentment is as sinful as whatever sin—and I mean *whatever sin*—the other person has committed.

Sisters, we have to let it go. If we don't, we can expect our family unit to wither away. Whatever wrong a husband has done, whatever mistake a child has made, let me say with every ounce of my soul (and you know I love you dearly)—you're killing yourself and your family. More than four hundred Americans die each year from carbon monoxide poisoning. I wonder how many thousands of families are destroyed because someone can't forgive.

We have to decide if holding on to the pain is worth waking up one day to find our families gone.

If you refuse to forgive others, your Father will not forgive your sins. MATTHEW 6:15

In the end, we must honestly ask the question: What is killing our family? The original sin and its wounds or the toxic gas of bitterness?

WHAT YOU WORRY ABOUT THAT YOU SHOULDN'T

WE'VE ESTABLISHED that as moms we're a stressed-out bunch. We agree that, from time to time, we tend to wander (or sometimes get completely lost) in a wilderness. We've explored opportunities to improve the state of our souls and affirm the value of our witness. Hopefully, this leads us to the place of Perfect Motherhood. Right?

Hmm . . . probably not. We'll never achieve perfection in our mothering role, and unless we lock our kids in the closet, it's important to note that we probably won't break them either.

I should know.

My mom fought and sometimes lost her battle with the beast of bipolar disorder. Her prescription drug consumption (Valium) was classic for the sixties and seventies. In her last years, alcohol became her escape. Even on a good day, her judgment could be impaired. She sometimes drove me crazy, but she didn't break me. She made me.

Despite the areas of her character that were weakened by her illness, I thrived because of the first and most important lesson she taught me: Jesus loves me. Furthermore, I knew *she* loved me, as did my father and grandmother. My family had me in church every Sunday morning, every Wednesday evening, and in my teenage years, every Sunday evening as well. As a result, the day Mom attempted suicide when I was just a teenager, Christ filled that gaping wound in a way no other could. The foundation of our family's love, coupled with knowing Christ's profound love for me, made a whole lot of wrong all right.

Looking back on my own years of parenting, I remember worrying constantly: *Am I being too strict? Am I being too lenient? Am I pushing too hard, expecting too much? Maybe I'm not expecting enough? Should I get involved in this? Should I give them space?* The sound track playing through my head never stopped, and no matter which song was playing, it never felt like the right tune.

If your kiddos are between the ages of twelve and twenty-one, you might have this score running through your headphones too. You worry you're gonna really mess them up. But I think you're worrying about something that you shouldn't. Why? Because you taught them that Jesus loves them, and they were his long before they were yours.

> I give them eternal life, and they will never perish. No one can snatch them away from me, for my Father has given them to me, and he is more powerful than anyone else. No one can snatch them from the Father's hand. The Father and I are one. **JOHN 10:28-30**

Now that you've put that out of your mind, worry about something that you *can* do something about—like that chicken that's been thawing in your fridge since Monday.

PRAY THIS,
NOT THAT, WITH THEM

"Mom, I hurt so bad."

Both of my children suffered the emotional pain of social exclusion, and there's a good chance one or more of your kiddos will enter this agonizing, lonely place over the course of their lifetime too. You will lie down with them, hold them in your arms, and comfort them as they weep, all while letting out tears of your own. It hurts so bad.

Isolation or exclusion is a different kind of hurt, and thanks to social media, never have our children been more susceptible to the butchering.

Numerous studies have been conducted over the years to understand why the areas of our brain that fire up when we experience physical pain also become active when we feel we have been socially excluded. In their article "Why Does Social Exclusion Hurt? The Relationship between Social and Physical Pain," Geoff MacDonald and Mark R. Leary include this statement: "Many people would prefer to be hit than ostracized, suggesting that the pain of social exclusion may be more aversive than the pain of physical injury."[18]

Based on the hours I spent holding my crying children or teens while working to rebuild and fortify their self-esteem, these studies confirm what I suspected: My children were being crushed.

During those difficult hours, I prayed for rescue—for a

friend to come to their aid. I prayed for intervention—for a new class or hobby or teacher to move them to a new social circle. I prayed for their protection—that the mean and spiteful kids wouldn't do permanent damage to their psyches. I even prayed with my kids, asking God to change the hearts of those who had made them feel like outcasts. And sometimes these prayers were answered according to our petition. But if I could go back in time, I would have prayed for something different. I would have prayed for my children's transformation.

A transformation of their hearts: to hurt less for themselves and more for their oppressors. A transformation of their minds: moving themselves intellectually from victim to victor. A transformation of their souls: from feeling alone to knowing they were protected and empowered by the Holy God of Israel. During those long, sad nights, I would have prayed this Scripture with them:

> I have called you by name; you are mine. When you go through deep waters, I will be with you. When you go through rivers of difficulty, you will not drown. When you walk through the fire of oppression, you will not be burned up; the flames will not consume you. For I am the LORD, your God, the Holy One of Israel, your Savior. ISAIAH 43:1-3

Yes. I would have prayed this.

FROM BAD TO WORSE

I AWOKE WITH A SPLITTING HEADACHE and a slight fever; I knew for sure I was coming down with something. But as a single mom at the time, there was no way I could stay home. I couldn't take the time unpaid because I was barely scraping by. Supporting the kids all on my own, I needed every nickel I had for rent and groceries. While I had some personal time stored up, I didn't want to dip into it, knowing it was only a matter of time before one of the kids came down with something and I'd need that benefit time to stay home with them. So after prying myself from my bed and getting all of us ready and out the door, I went to the office, taking a break every couple of hours to lie down on the floor in the fetal position. I was sick as a dog.

As if my fever and pounding headache were not enough, it was also one of the coldest weeks on record in Dallas; overnight temperatures were dropping into the low single digits. The heater in our house couldn't keep up, so I had no choice but to call a repairman I knew through another friend. Taking pity on my situation, he discounted the service call to sixty dollars—which was great—but when two hundred dollars is all you have to your name, it's still a large amount. The good news/bad news on the heater was that there was nothing wrong with it. It was working to full capacity, and this was just the way it would be until the weather warmed up. Great. We were living in a warm refrigerator.

You know this story is going to get worse, right? Yes, ma'am. Scott caught my bug and needed to go to the doctor. Oh, my. I would now dip into the little reserves I had left for the co-pay. But thank God for his provision that I could. And I did.

I have a soft spot in my heart for you single moms because I know how hard your job is—and how often things seem to go from bad to worse.

You likely work a stressful job by day and clean, do laundry, and help with homework by night. You shop and cook dinner, but you also mow and tend to your lawn. You wash your own car, have the oil and tires changed, and you personally deal with every light bulb, every smoke alarm, and every appliance that goes on the fritz. You switch seamlessly (but stressfully) from your mommy role one minute—soothing hurts or playing games—to being the dad the next, emphatically setting boundaries and sticking to them.

When you want to cry, you don't because you can't afford the time or the emotional expenditure. There's too much to do, and everyone is counting on you.

> Turn to me and have mercy, for I am alone and in deep distress. My problems go from bad to worse. Oh, save me from them all! Feel my pain and see my trouble. Forgive all my sins. **PSALM 25:16-18**

You likely feel alone. Sweet friend, you're not. Hold on. I'm praying for you.

THE BALD GUY IN YOUR BED

IT WAS OUR FIRST CHRISTMAS together as a family of four. Steve asked me if there was anything special I wanted. Without hesitation I answered, "Yes! I want you to shave your beard."

In all the time I had known him and in all the pictures I had seen of him as an adult, he had always had a beard. I wanted to see Steve's face. Of course he protested. He'd had his beard since he was eighteen years old, and though he loved me dearly, he was clear that he had no intention of shaving it off. *Okay, fine. How about a mixer, then?*

The kids were nine and twelve when we married and were still prone to waking up way too early to see what Santa had delivered. Always trying to stay one step ahead of them, I woke up early on Christmas to wash my face and prepare for the celebration. As I rolled over to kiss Steve good morning, the filtered light of dawn streamed through our window blinds, slightly distorting his face. As my hand touched his cheek—I shot up in bed and screamed.

Steve had gotten up in the middle of the night, gone across the house to the guest bath, shaved his beard, and crawled silently back into bed.

My first thought that morning was *Who is in my bed?*

My realization of his "surprise gift" ended in giddy laughter (and a flipping on of the lamp!). I could see my husband's face for the first time.

Many women my age wake up after twenty-five years of marriage in bed with a total stranger—often some bald guy. Oh, they know his name and his birthday. They know all of his bad habits. They know his favorite foods and what ticks him off.

But they've forgotten to *see* him as they've busied themselves with everything and everyone else vying for their attention. His face has become distorted, and over the years these women have failed to caress his cheek or head to ask, "What happened to your hair?"

Sweet moms, please don't lose your connection with your husbands. When you wake up with your bald guy, I pray you will be giddy with laughter at the love God has blessed you with.

Draw me after you and let us run together!
SONG OF SOLOMON 1:4, NASB

The best years of your marriage are yet to come. Take a good look at him tonight . . . while he still has hair.

PRAY THIS, NOT THAT, FOR HIM

As we explore how we pray and whom we pray for, there's another person we need to add to our prayer list, isn't there? We often know how to pray for ourselves and our children, but I wonder if we really know how to pray for our husbands. That is—a prayer that is not self-serving. Uh-oh.

I don't know a couple, Steve and me included, who have not experienced challenges when it comes to determining what is "best for the kids." Sitting on opposing sides of the parenting strategy is really tough on a marriage: Do we bribe or threaten? How should we discipline? Does their behavior really merit a reward? And for parents with children who have ADHD—do we medicate or not? Both parents want the same outcome: a self-motivated, kind, self-sufficient kid. But sometimes the divergent roads available to get there can be hard to navigate.

I think many of us are tempted to pray that God will bring our husbands around to our way of thinking. We're so sure we have the solution to the problem figured out—if only he'd just play along! Over the years, I slowly learned that my way is often not the best way. I have learned not to pray for Steve to come to my way of thinking, but to ask for God's divine intervention to press on his heart what is best and right—and then to align my heart with his. Whether we're dealing with small issues or a major crisis, we know that a house divided will fall (Mark 3:25).

Many parents who are just starting out or who have wayward teens find their marriages in turmoil because they cannot align their courses or strategies for parenting. Their styles, their timing, and often their own upbringings conflict, turning an already complex job into a high-stakes wrestling match. Good grief! Like getting this kid raised is not hard enough!

Rather than pray for him to see things your way, pray for God's intervention so your husband will be blessed with wisdom and leadership—and so that God's will might be done. This may test your humility to no end so pray that you both can keep open minds and open hearts. And pray for guidance to help you to start acting as the "one" you are.

> For this reason a man shall leave his father and his mother, and be joined to his wife; and they shall become one flesh.
> **GENESIS 2:24, NASB**

That sweet little four-year-old coloring at the coffee table looks innocent enough now but will one day be a formidable foe. United today in preparation for the battle tomorrow.

YOUR TIME CAPSULE

I HAVE SEVERAL TIME CAPSULES in our garage. Actually, they're Rubbermaid plastic bins packed with keepsakes from my mother, father, and grandmother. Together they represent an era between the late 1800s and 1997. Inside them are the remaining earthly items I have to remember my family.

They contain a wide variety of treasures—from a teeny-tiny knife my paternal grandmother used to cut buttonholes and Daddy's watch that I worked, saved, and bought for him when I was in high school to my grandmother's valedictorian speech and the cross Mom was wearing the night she died.

But of all these items, none is more revealing of any one of their characters than the hundreds of processed checks my grandmother kept. Yes, I'm a dork for keeping them, too, but they show just how she spent her money and what she valued.

Of all of the checks she wrote, Mammaw's weekly tithe to the First Baptist Church of Bells, Texas, tickles me most. She gave a three-dollar sacrifice every week. I mean every week. There are hundreds of them! In her time capsule I am reminded of her faithfulness, her stewardship, and her fastidious bookkeeping.

I think about the things my kids might keep to remember me. Would they want a Toni permanent solution kit to remind them of that terrible smell in the seventies when I was going for a blonde Donna Summer look? Would they save the white jumpsuit I wore one Christmas that they called my astronaut suit? (It was very hip for the time.) I'm sure they'd hold on to my needles and thread. (As Ava declared last week when she needed a patch sewn onto her soccer jersey, "Thank heavens someone in this family knows how to sew!") I imagine my cookbooks, business books, and yoga mat might remind them of my very varied interests, from things domestic to professional to wacky.

I do hope one of them wants my Bible. With notes written in nearly every margin and pages dimpled by tears, it is worn and read through and through going on nearly thirty years. I hope that for my children, the words written in my Bible will define me and my longing to know him more than any other item in their Rubbermaid time capsule remembrance box of me.

> He issued his laws to Jacob; he gave his instructions to Israel. He commanded our ancestors to teach them to their children, so the next generation might know them— even the children not yet born—and they in turn will teach their own children. **PSALM 78:5-6**

What will your kids put in a time capsule to remember you? Your legacy box is being assembled as you read.

In the meantime, be careful what you wear. They'll never let you live it down.

IT'S A PRESSURE COOKER

I DON'T HAVE A PRESSURE COOKER, but my parents did. I was always intrigued by the metronome-like noise that indicated it was working (and dinner would be ready soon) and the clearly expressed danger of removing the steam regulator too early.

If you're not familiar with how a pressure cooker works, broth or other liquid builds steam that is sealed inside a specially designed, airtight pot. The vapor increases the pressure inside the pot along with the maximum temperature that the liquid can reach, infusing the broth or other liquid into the food. And it all happens very fast. Did you get that there is an element of danger?

Some of our kids are a bit like little pressure cookers. A whole lot is going on beneath their seal, and one little trip of the regulator can result in disaster. Here's what's scary: This is happening to highly intelligent, sweet, awesome kids attending our top public and private high schools and our finest universities.

It's sad that *stressed-out* might best define today's generation of high-achieving teens. Statistics are often hollow without relevancy, so let's look at the facts[19] in a hypothetical situation:

Imagine you have a nineteen-year-old daughter, Cassi, who attends Dr. Anderson's Human Biology 201 lecture every Tuesday and Thursday at 9:30 a.m. She sits in the auditorium with 399 other kids. She is one of the 339 who feel overwhelmed on a daily basis. Keeping up with her workload and grades while managing the land mines of her always-on, complex social network has her stressed out and often on the verge of tears. What she hasn't told you is that she is among the fifty-two of her fellow Human Biology classmates who have been officially diagnosed with a mental health condition such as anxiety or depression—in her case, by her school's counseling center. If you don't know this, then you also don't know that she's among the thirty-six students sitting in class this morning who have seriously considered suicide this year.

Data gets more real when it's our kids.

As I visited with a college administrator of a major university recently, he told me that students today, especially freshmen, are completely overwhelmed and are ending up in the ER at an alarming rate. *Often because they have received their first B.*

The kids in our modern families are amped up on success, prestige, and recognition. When they can't keep up the pace or the face of accomplishment, the pressure builds.

Jesus said, "Come to me, all of you who are weary and carry heavy burdens, and I will give you rest. Take my yoke upon you. Let me teach you, because I am humble and gentle at heart, and you will find rest for your souls. For my yoke is easy to bear, and the burden I give you is light." **MATTHEW 11:28-30**

Not once in the Bible does Christ favor the manically driven or obsessed. Moms, make sure those babies know where they can off-load that backpack of burden. Especially when they get a B.

W.D.C.D.
(WHAT DID CARLOTTA DO?)

FAILURE TO LAUNCH. That's today's buzz line for young adults who enter the workforce ill-prepared and end up back home living in their parents' basement. The struggle of this newest generation to gain traction in the workplace falls on us all to address.

Mom, you have no idea how important you are to our economy. From small-business owners to Fortune 100 professionals, we depend on you to help prepare our future employees. Whether you are parenting a millennial or a generation Z-er (Lord, help us!), you are ground zero. You establish for them a solid foundation on which companies like mine look to build.

We're doing better, but the workplace was not and still is not completely prepared for this newest generation of workers—and we have learned that many of them are still not prepared for us. There is a disconnect between some of our newest job seekers and the harsh realities of a competitive marketplace. But please don't think that all young adults of this generation are ill-equipped, because they're not. Let me introduce you to a very successful millennial.

After completing high school near the top of her class, Phoebe then earned a degree from the University of Texas. She's very smart. But so are a lot of other millennials who have come through our firm's doors only to flame out.

I have marveled at Phoebe's emotional intelligence, her work ethic, and her ability to perform her duties with focus and excellence. Good grades alone didn't prepare Phoebe for success. My suspicion was that her mom, Carlotta, was somehow responsible. And I was right. So you're probably asking yourself . . .

What did Carlotta do?

I warn you this is not easy. It's hard work to help your kids develop a great work ethic beyond the classroom. But it's going to be hard to do their laundry again when they're twenty-six, so read on . . .

Carlotta consistently held Phoebe accountable. Phoebe didn't just do chores—Carlotta checked the work to ensure that they were done correctly. A dish that wasn't washed well went back in the sink. Carlotta inspected what she expected. She instilled in Phoebe from a very early age that it's not enough to do a job and check the box—a job done poorly would have to be done over. Moms, this is a concept lost on many in this generation. They have yet to learn how to hold themselves accountable for anything outside of making an "A" because no one else has.

In addition, Phoebe was required to earn her own spending money, so she held a part-time summer job. Juggling her summer reading assignments with her chores (done well) and her part-time work, Phoebe became hardwired to plan strategically and work efficiently.

Carlotta, goal driven herself, provided an example to Phoebe by putting herself through college and starting her own business. Phoebe had a front-row seat to witness how determination and hard work pay off. This gave Phoebe a competitive edge among her peers; she knows nothing will be handed to her. In the marketplace, accolades, raises, and promotions are hard earned. This is lost on some of our millennials.

Lastly, let me share with you sweet moms that expressed appreciation is still in vogue in the marketplace. Phoebe has mastered this, too, thanking her supervisors whenever she receives compliments, bonuses, raises, or other perks. In fact, she is better at this than many coworkers with much more work experience.

> Start children off on the way they should go, and even when they are old they will not turn from it.
> **PROVERBS 22:6, NIV**

You want your kids off your payroll. I want them on mine. When in doubt in preparing them for the future, ask yourself, W.D.C.D.? Thank you, Mom. Your hard work benefits us all.

THE MAKING
OF A DISCONTENT

BESIDES A FEW SHORT-RUN RECESSIONS, our society has never known a time of serious economic distress—at least not to the point of what previous generations experienced after the stock market crash of '29 or during World War II. Compared to our grandparents and great-grandparents, we live in a state of abundance.

But we often act like we have no time or money to spare. The further away from misfortune we ride, the less we seem to value our blessings. Many of us are oblivious to the fact that we have all we could possibly ever need. A failure to recognize our abundance gives way to a perceived need or longing for more. Longing for more gives way to self-indulgence. Self-indulgence leads to greediness. Greediness and the desire to obtain more bring us to a state of total discontentment.

If you look to instill a sense of *longing for more* in your children, I think I have the perfect ten-step plan. It's critical to follow the instructions in their entirety. Please don't skip a step.

1. *Argue.* Focus all of your disagreements or arguments on money—especially when discussing what you want, need, or don't have. This will ensure that your child understands there is always something else to long for and value more than harmony.

2. *Entertain.* Engage only in family entertainment that requires money. Picnics, game nights, cooking together, and other free activities should be avoided.

3. *Indulge.* Give your children everything they want, when they want it. And when they get it, don't express your displeasure if they soon cast it aside.

4. *Entitle.* Never make your children do chores to earn money. And whatever you do, don't require your teens to have a part-time summer job. Children should focus only on fun and grades.

5. *Focus.* Ensure that every conversation you have over dinner turns to spending or saving money. Don't discuss topics of generosity, those in need, or charitable giving. That will put all kinds of crazy ideas in your kids' heads.

6. *Hoard.* Please don't let them see you give your money away. Don't tithe or give to charitable organizations. Don't even discuss what sacrifices you might make as a family to contribute to others. Keep every dollar to yourselves.

7. *Compensate.* If you do tithe, make sure you give money to your kids to drop in the plate. If you want them to be true discontents, they should never know the joy of earning and giving their own money.

8. *Guilt.* Make sure your kids feel bad when something they truly do need is expensive—especially child care, school clothes, and fees for school outings. This ensures they will feel guilty and continue to live in a state of scarcity long after you're dead and gone.

9. *Be scarce.* Live like you're afraid you won't have dinner tomorrow night. This has a profound impact on kids

and sometimes helps them to hoard their money later in life.

10. *Be unappreciative.* Never, ever say grace. Don't mention the fabulous riches of salvation, nature, the miracle of God's daily provision, or the abundant gift of love and family he has blessed you with. You'll never have a discontent if you talk about blessings.

There you have it! Children guaranteed to grow into adults who will never be happy—people so wrapped up in their longing for more that they never know the joy of giving. Discontent bathed in scarcity.

> Give, and you will receive. Your gift will return to you in full—pressed down, shaken together to make room for more, running over, and poured into your lap. The amount you give will determine the amount you get back.
> **LUKE 6:38**

Not looking to raise spoiled, entitled brats? Ensure for your children a great return of blessings on *their* investment in others, and they'll always live in a state of abundance.

I WANNA BE LIKE ME

SOME OF MY CONTEMPORARIES and I made a mistake: We overshot our influence. It is not a parenting miss isolated to our generation. For ages, parents have overdirected.

It's an easy trap for many parents to fall into because we want the best for our children. But for all our good intentions—earthly wisdom and keen insight into what we think will make our children happy (and make us *really* happy)—we can be wrong. Too easily we meddle with God's plan.

It starts when we register them for pre-K and persists even when they declare a major in college. From soccer to basketball, from dance to violin, from an interest in bugs to an obsession with rocks—we meddle. We cajole, we bribe, we trade to get our little darlings exposed and interested in sports, subjects, and the arts in which we'd love to see them excel. Our pride, the promise of scholarships, or just a mutual hobby or interest can drive the "recommendation." Sometimes it's something we wanted to do as a child but couldn't—so we imprint our desires onto our kids, only to watch them dig trenches in the sand while playing center field or pick their noses in the spotlight while dressed in pink tutus.

In an effort to help our children navigate their professional waters, some of us direct our children to careers we feel will be rewarding—especially *financially* rewarding. We exercise our influence by encouraging career paths and associated majors that will pay more over those that might actually be more fulfilling and meaningful or align better with their natural abilities or interests. We even direct them to our own fields in hopes they will one day take over the family business or practice, only to watch them burn out or die a slow, agonizing professional death due to boredom.

So is that what God has in store for them? Is that what he has written on their hearts?

I'm afraid our children, especially those who have toed the line, made good grades, and are prone to "please," allow undue influence to the parents they love so dearly. Sometimes they acquiesce because they are young and confused. But some have just yet to find their voices to articulate what they feel. Perhaps Sara Bareilles, in her song "I Wanna Be like Me," has said it for them: "What if I don't wanna be like you? . . . I was made to be exactly like me."[20]

> Thank you for making me so wonderfully complex!
> Your workmanship is marvelous—how well I know it.
> **PSALM 139:14**

Help them find their voices rather than their professions. If they hate taking piano today, they'll probably still hate it next year.

ATYPICALLY TYPICAL

THE TV SITCOM *Modern Family* introduced viewers to an atypically typical American family. Many Christians were appalled. I was actually comforted.

My first modern family would have made for a fabulous television show. My twenty-nine-year-old, trophy-wife, platinum-blonde bombshell of a mother and my gray-haired fifty-five-year-old father must have been the talk of the hospital as they welcomed their daughter to the world in 1959. With three half sisters my mom's age or older and a half brother from my mom's previous marriage (to a man who came out of the closet after she was pregnant in 1951!), we were a "blended" family. Unfortunately, there was no tasteful moniker for us during my early days. We were just weird.

But I learned it didn't matter. We were loved, and we loved Jesus.

My own family is also atypical. After my first marriage failed, I remarried. Steve adopted Shauna and Scott as teenagers. Scott, having been adopted at four months, was adopted a second time at thirteen. How many kids do you know who were adopted twice? Scott is gay, which adds to our ongoing atypically typical family.

While Shauna was picking up her passport one day, eight-year-old Ava listened intently to the conversation between her mom and the clerk. As Shauna answered the clerk's questions, Ava corrected her mother as she gave the administrator her birth name. When Shauna shushed her, Ava insisted to the administrator that her mother hailed from the Miller clan. (Needless to say, this caused some short-term concern on the clerk's part as to who was telling the truth.) After clearing up the matter and breaking free of the administrator's suspicious look of confusion, Shauna took Ava to Starbucks. It was time to come clean.

"Sugar was married before Poppy? So what else have you not told me?" Ava was incredulous.

A hundred stories ran through Shauna's head—everything from her own heartbreaking disappointments to disclosing the true origin of Lucy, their Elf on the Shelf. But this was enough for one day.

"That's everything," Shauna said. Everything, except our family is anything but normal.

Your modern family might not be typical either. You might be a stepmom or a single mom. You might be a mom to mixed-race children, to foster children, or to children adopted from other countries. You might be a mom who is judged or scorned by others because you don't fit the mold.

This truth remains: Jesus loves you, and if you love him, he welcomes you as his child.

> Now you Gentiles are no longer strangers and foreigners. You are citizens along with all of God's holy people. You are members of God's family. **EPHESIANS 2:19**

God's family is about as atypical as it gets. And you know what's really great? You are loved.

WHAT YOU DON'T PRAY FOR THAT YOU SHOULD

Most things we worry about are not worthy of the time and energy we invest or the peace we forfeit. Isn't it amazing how most things just work out? I love the quote by Joseph Crossman: "If you want to test your memory, try to recall what you were worrying about one year ago today." Shoot. I can't remember what I was worrying about last month! Wouldn't you love to get back those hours of sleepless nights and those days and waves of nausea? And what about those endless *what-if* tapes that play through your head? I would love to get all that time back.

There are even some prayers I would rescind if I could. I can't believe all the things I have prayed for that were so temporal—solutions to rescue my family or myself for a day, a month, or even a year—when, in fact, I should have been praying for things that would have a lifelong and eternal impact.

If I could go back in time to the days when the kids were just babes, I would pray day and night that my children would fall hopelessly in love with Christ. Oh, I prayed that they would accept Christ as their Savior and I prayed that they would walk in his truth. But I never thought to petition the Holy Spirit to kindle a love affair deep within their being for their Savior.

Many of us begin praying for our baby's spouse as we

rock them at night. I remember praying for Adam (of course, I didn't know it was Adam) when Shauna was just a few months old. We often pray for their earthly mates, but I don't think we spend enough time on our knees praying for their devotion to their *eternal mate*.

Regardless of how young or old our children are, what challenges they may face, and what fabulous dreams may come true for them, their deep, abiding love for Jesus Christ will be the most defining thing about their character. Their intimate knowledge of him; their understanding and acceptance of his abounding, unconditional love; and their conviction to follow him will pave their way through this world to the next. Having a passion for Christ enables our children to live a life of hope, to operate in a place of peace, to serve with a spirit of love, and to live a life of joy regardless of what comes their way.

> That is what the Scriptures mean when they say, "No eye has seen, no ear has heard, and no mind has imagined what God has prepared for those who love him."
> 1 CORINTHIANS 2:9

I didn't think to pray this for my children when they were young. Only now has it really been on my heart, but the good news is that it is never too late. We want blessings for our children, and what he desires to give them is beyond our wildest imagination. Pray for the love affair that will last eternity.

day 88

BLINDSIDED

I WANT TO LOVE ON YOU MOMS who have experienced heartbreak as the result of a wayward child. I know firsthand your pain. Although our parenting was far from perfect, Steve and I were pretty sure as we were raising those kids that we were doing most things "right." We followed God's Word. We invested in our children. We prayed. We corrected. We believed. Still . . .

Some things are out of our control.

A number of us have been blindsided. Some of us have been completely coldcocked. We have suffered the anxiety, outrage, confusion, shame, and despair that follow the fallout from our children's devastatingly poor choices. When we lose them to *their wilderness*, we might as well be walking in the desert too.

If you're a mom who is in a tough place where you don't understand what he is thinking, can't reach her to know what she's feeling, and can't possibly fathom why he's doing what he's doing or why she can't see the disastrous path she's on, I hope you will hold on to this:

Our God is good . . . even when our children are terribly wrong. God, in his glorious mercy, redeems pain and sin and heartbreak in the most creative of ways, especially when we choose to walk through the most difficult and heartbreaking situations with him. Only when we give up on God's goodness, doubt his grace, and discount his love do we fail to recognize his greater purpose in the pain.

> We know that God causes everything to work together for the good of those who love God and are called according to his purpose for them. **ROMANS 8:28**

When you run out of ideas, out of prayers, and out of patience, you can trust he's got this. Even as horrible as it is.

THE COVENANT

AT OUR COMPANY we have some hard-and-fast rules. These tenets guide our teams to ensure there is no ambiguity as to what we expect, what excellence looks like, or what we value.

To raise Christian kids in a secular world (and not lose your marbles), you need a set of hard-and-fast rules, too. You can do this "Moses style" and present these principles to your kids on stone tablets, or you can just gather at the kitchen table and pen an agreement there . . . (However, I think chiseled tablets would be way cool and would definitely get everyone's attention.)

I wish I had thought to develop a covenant when our kids were young. Although they both knew the rules—since *they were often repeated*—there was no written documentation. We had no mutual covenant. And certainly there was no understanding when Shauna and Scott were preteens as to why this set of values was critical to their witness, our Christian code, or our family's honor. But if I had to develop them today, here are a few I'd chisel in the rock on our fireplace:

Honesty. We will believe you, and you can believe us. Trust is vital in our relationship, and to be clear, honesty includes full disclosure. Without honesty, the rest of the covenant falls apart. Should you lose our trust, its restoration will be hard-won. Our family is truthful with one another.

Acceptance. We will not judge you. You can tell us anything, and we will listen. We will not interrupt. We will hear you out, and we will help you out. Likewise, you will hear us out, too, and accept that our counsel is always given from a place of protection and love. Our family loves unconditionally.

Availability. We will be present in one another's company. Conversation will trump any and all electronic devices, social networks, and TV. This includes work interruptions that distract us from you. Our family is present in the moment.

Support. We will help one another. We will help you with your homework and school projects, and drive you wherever you need to be; you will help with taking out the trash, making your bed, and doing your laundry. Our family takes care of one another.

Inclusion. There are no cliques, favorites, or "sides" in our family. We are all for one and one for all. Everyone is treated equally, including each person having the opportunity to unload the dishwasher at least once a week. Our family is one unit. (Note: This applies even, *and especially*, if you're a blended family.)

Respect. We will respect and reward your good decisions as you grow. You will respect our position of authority and our wisdom to discern your "next steps." Our family is respectful in tone, word, and deed.

Honor. We are honored to have you as our child. You will honor your reputation, your body, and your Savior with your actions. When you do this, you also honor us. Our family honor will honor Christ.

Consequences. If you break this covenant, you can count on a consequence. We love you that much. Our family upholds and defends our boundaries.

This is the new covenant I will make with the people of Israel on that day, says the LORD: I will put my laws in their minds, and I will write them on their hearts. I will be their God, and they will be my people. **HEBREWS 8:10**

Put your own covenant in writing. Post it to the fridge. Be clear. Then stand firm. Mom, don't let them wear you down.

IF YOU ONLY REMEMBER THIS

RAISING KIDS IS EXHAUSTING.

Let's just admit it: Whether they're two or twenty, we are tempted to look the other way when we know something about their story doesn't smell right. We let our guard down when they appear to be on the straight and narrow (but we know in our hearts that this may be too good to be true). We pretend we didn't hear what they just said to their sister or notice something weird about that text. We even make excuses for them because we want so badly for them to straighten up and fly right! We're exhausted.

Two words for you, sweet mom: Be steadfast.

This is not a time for you to be a sissy, get tired, or be overconfident. The wolves of a dangerous, even deadly, secular world are howling at your door. Shoot! They may be prowling through the texts and pictures on your kid's cell phone as I write! I don't envy you. This is probably one of the most difficult generations to raise a child in decades. And it's not going to get any easier. So I'm praying for you. I am praying that you will remain steadfast.

Steadfast is not a word we commonly use today, but I love this word when I think of a quality that is key to keeping you strong as you parent. To be steadfast means you are unflinching—you are not going to blink and you won't back down. You stay on top of technology and one step ahead of them—you'll not be lulled or fooled. It means you are unwavering—you know what you are committed to, and you will not bow down to anything that is ungodly or harmful to your children's welfare; you embrace the word *no*. You will not succumb to the pull of culture and trends (no matter how much your children whine and pout) because you will do anything and everything to protect their emotional, mental, and spiritual well-being. To be steadfast is to be abiding—to wait, watch, suffer, and pray along with them. And to be steadfast is to be relentless. You are a *pit bull* when it comes to defending and raising your kids with Christian values. You. Are. On. It.

I cannot even fathom the complexity and challenges you will face over the next several years. But God can. And he's in your corner.

> My beloved brethren, be steadfast, immovable, always abounding in the work of the Lord, knowing that your labor is not in vain in the Lord. **1 CORINTHIANS 15:58**, NKJV

You're not just fighting the good fight—you're fighting the *best* fight. Be steadfast.

I SAID THIS PRAYER *for You* LAST NIGHT

Father, from the womb to the tomb we're all flawed, and you still receive us with such joy! As you accept, forgive, and extend grace to us, I pray for my sisters' households—that their homes will be cleansed of the poison of bitterness. Pour over each household a liberating spirit of forgiveness. Show each family the blessing that comes from extending grace.

I know every mom hurts for her children when they are being excluded or bullied. Bless their children with hearts, minds, and souls that are completely transformed from despair to victory. Make them new, whole, and completely confident in your almighty power.

I pray for the single moms who carry the load alone, that you will fortify them with energy, provision, and joy every day, but especially on those days when things go from bad to worse. I lift up those who have grown apart from their husbands. Give those couples love anew, and align their hearts and minds as one as they guide their children.

I pray the blessing of wisdom and discernment over this mom as she prepares her child for success in the world at large. Provide her the tools and resources to build a strong foundation for her family, to define and maintain boundaries, and to empower her children to find their voices and the confidence to use them. Open her children's hearts to your truths and direction as they navigate the sometimes murky and rough waters ahead.

*As she mothers in this exceedingly complex world, Father,
I pray you will reveal the truths you want for her and her family
and that you will equip her to instill a spirit of generosity and
abundance in her child.*

*If this mom is anxious, angry, confused, shamed, heart-
broken, or in complete despair, Father, I pray you will comfort
her. Remind her, moment by moment, that you're in charge,
that you've got this, and that your grace and mercy are all
she needs.*

*Keep her steadfast. Don't let her waver. Don't let her relent.
Keep her as your watchdog over your children. Lord, don't let
them wear her down.*

Amen.

POWER TOOLS

I HAVE SOME AWESOME power tools. I keep them in the kitchen.

There's not a "man's" tool in the world that can hold a candle to my KitchenAid mixer. That baby can mix a batch of Parker House rolls, and I never break a sweat. My KitchenAid mixer is the bomb.

I have a plastic juicer that I bought at the dollar store. It's cheap, but man, does that baby do the job. I can juice a lemon and strain the seeds in seconds. It delivers.

My zester. My Zojirushi rice cooker. And this funny little tool my mother-in-law gave me to loosen and pop jar lids. These all save my bacon.

While I depend on my basic pots and pans for most of my cooking, when I'm in a pinch or if something special is happening in the kitchen, I know I can depend on my power tools.

God's Word is my power tool too. When life gets hard or there's some unique challenge in front of me, I depend on his counsel, his comfort, and his love. This power tool isn't stored in my cabinets, but in my heart. I hope you will add these to your collection too.

God arms me with strength, and he makes my way perfect.
PSALM 18:32

Put on every piece of God's armor so you will be able to resist the enemy in the time of evil. Then after the battle you will still be standing firm. **EPHESIANS 6:13**

Here am I, and the children the LORD has given me. We are signs and symbols in Israel from the LORD Almighty, who dwells on Mount Zion. **ISAIAH 8:18, NIV**

May God, who gives this patience and encouragement, help you live in complete harmony with each other, as is fitting for followers of Christ Jesus. **ROMANS 15:5**

If you refuse to forgive others, your Father will not forgive your sins. **MATTHEW 6:15**

I give them eternal life, and they will never perish. No one can snatch them away from me, for my Father has given them to me, and he is more powerful than anyone else. No one can snatch them from the Father's hand. The Father and I are one. **JOHN 10:28-30**

I have called you by name; you are mine. When you go through deep waters, I will be with you. When you go through rivers of difficulty, you will not drown. When you walk through the fire of oppression, you will not be burned up; the flames will not consume you. For I am the LORD, your God, the Holy One of Israel, your Savior. **ISAIAH 43:1-3**

Turn to me and have mercy, for I am alone and in deep distress. My problems go from bad to worse. Oh, save me from them all! Feel my pain and see my trouble. Forgive all my sins. **PSALM 25:16-18**

Draw me after you and let us run together!
SONG OF SOLOMON 1:4, NASB

For this reason a man shall leave his father and his mother, and be joined to his wife; and they shall become one flesh.
GENESIS 2:24, NASB

He issued his laws to Jacob; he gave his instructions to Israel. He commanded our ancestors to teach them to their children, so the next generation might know them—even the children not yet born—and they in turn will teach their own children. **PSALM 78:5-6**

Jesus said, "Come to me, all of you who are weary and carry heavy burdens, and I will give you rest. Take my yoke upon

you. Let me teach you, because I am humble and gentle at heart, and you will find rest for your souls. For my yoke is easy to bear, and the burden I give you is light."
MATTHEW 11:28-30

Start children off on the way they should go, and even when they are old they will not turn from it. **PROVERBS 22:6, NIV**

Give, and you will receive. Your gift will return to you in full—pressed down, shaken together to make room for more, running over, and poured into your lap. The amount you give will determine the amount you get back. **LUKE 6:38**

Thank you for making me so wonderfully complex! Your workmanship is marvelous—how well I know it. **PSALM 139:14**

Now you Gentiles are no longer strangers and foreigners. You are citizens along with all of God's holy people. You are members of God's family. **EPHESIANS 2:19**

That is what the Scriptures mean when they say, "No eye has seen, no ear has heard, and no mind has imagined what God has prepared for those who love him." **1 CORINTHIANS 2:9**

We know that God causes everything to work together for the good of those who love God and are called according to his purpose for them. **ROMANS 8:28**

This is the new covenant I will make with the people of Israel on that day, says the LORD: I will put my laws in their minds, and I will write them on their hearts. I will be their God, and they will be my people. **HEBREWS 8:10**

My beloved brethren, be steadfast, immovable, always abounding in the work of the Lord, knowing that your labor is not in vain in the Lord. **1 CORINTHIANS 15:58, NKJV**

Acknowledgments

BEFORE I EVER THOUGHT about writing and publishing a book, I guessed that the practice of authorship was a solitary endeavor. I surmised that writers were blessed with an exceptional idea and—with creative juices flowing—simply sat down at their computers and allowed their captivating and inspiring words to fill the pages. Of course, I also thought that accompanying this burst of genius came the naturally possessed grammar and composition skills of my high school English teacher, Mrs. Griffin.

Having completed my second book, I can safely report that this accomplishment is anything but a solo act. It was a collaborative adventure in which multiple characters arrived on the scene at just the right moment, perfectly illustrating God's provision.

Years before I conceived of *Lord, Have Mercy*, my husband, Steve, encouraged me repeatedly to write another book. By peppering me with questions, engaging me in conversations on various topics, and expressing his confidence in me, he sparked a fire that became a burning conviction to write again. Steve, there are no words to express my love for you and adoration for your abiding support in all I attempt.

It's one thing to write about a topic on which you are well-versed; it's something else to be inspired. For that, I thank my daughter, Shauna, for her selfless contribution—from brainstorming ideas to "speaking the truth in love" as we reviewed various drafts. Shauna, I am blessed beyond measure to be your mom, and I know I can always rely on your honest (and often hilarious) assessment, as well as your generous advice to bring greater clarity to my projects.

We all need an "old soul" in our lives; mine just happens to be in the form of my eight-year-old granddaughter. Thank you, my sweet Ava, for the joy you bring to our every conversation. Your thoughtful questions, wise observations, and sweet-spirited correction make me a better wife, mother, grandmother, and daughter of the King.

I suspect most authors appreciate their editors. I *cherish* mine. Kim Miller and Sarah Kelley are my walking-talking, grammar-correcting, research-perfecting, lovingly examining editors who make me look smarter than I am. Their counsel and direction provided in such a God-honoring manner made what could have been a frustrating experience on this journey, one of enlightenment and delight. I thank my grammar police from the bottom of my heart for their professional courtesy and dedication to excellence.

But the key characters I would like to honor in this book adventure are God the Father, Jesus Christ, and the Holy Spirit. I praise them for their favor in allowing me to write of their love in a short-story format, for the tugging on my heart to write on these specific topics, and for the blessing of *our* divine appointment. Lord, have mercy—*God is so good.*

ELLEN MILLER is the author of *The One Year Book of Inspiration for Girlfriends . . . Juggling Not-So-Perfect, Often-Crazy, but Gloriously Real Lives*. She is the founder of Insider Marketing and has served as its CEO since 1994. The company is known for launching some of the most important technologies and products of our time for Global 100 technology brands.

Living in Dallas, Ellen enjoys life to the fullest with her husband, Steve, as well as their two grown children, son-in-law, and granddaughter.

May the love of God fill your heart as you love others.
May the will of God fill your mind as you discern your way.
And may the peace of God cover you and yours . . . from head to toe!

Endnotes

1. Kathryn Stockett, *The Help* (New York: Berkley, 2011), 521.
2. Oswald Chambers, *Run Today's Race: A Word from Oswald Chambers for Every Day* (Grand Rapids, MI: Discovery House, 2015), August 23 entry.
3. Mark Niesse, "92-Year-Old Marathoner's Secret? 'Think Positive,'" NBCNews .com, April 5, 2011, http://www.nbcnews.com/id/42427918/ns/us_news -life/t/-year-old-marathoners-secret-think-positive/#.WFxRjGozXq4; Alissa Greenberg, "This 92-Year-Old Is the Oldest Woman to Ever Run (and Finish) a Marathon," Time.com, June 1, 2015, http://time.com/3902968/marathon -oldest-woman-harriette-thompson-cancer/; George Owens, "Syracuse University Alumna Harriette Thompson, 92, Becomes Oldest Woman to Finish Marathon," Syracuse.com, May 31, 2015, http://www.syracuse.com/news/index.ssf/2015/05 /oldest_female_marathon_finisher_harriette_thompson_syracuse_university_san _diego.html.
4. Alice O'Grady and Frances Throop, *The Story Teller's Book* (Chicago: Rand McNally & Co., 1912), 75.
5. "Train Rescue: Commuters Use People Power to Free Man Trapped against Platform at Perth's Stirling Station," ABC News Australia, August 6, 2014, http://www.abc.net.au/news/2014-08-06/man-freed-after-leg-trapped-in-gap -on-perth-train-station/5652486.
6. C. S. Lewis, *Mere Christianity* (New York: HarperCollins, 2001), 205.
7. Dr. Jim Denison, "Principal Dies Saving the Children She Served," Denison Forum on Truth and Culture, January 28, 2016, https://www.denisonforum.org /columns/cultural-commentary/principal-dies-saving-the-children-she-served.
8. "Yom Kippur—Day of Atonement," ReformJudaism.org, http://www.reform judaism.org/jewish-holidays/yom-kippur-day-atonement.
9. "People Check Their Smartphones 85 Times a Day (and They Don't Even Know They're Doing It)," press release, Nottingham Trent University, November 2, 2015, http://www4.ntu.ac.uk/apps/news/180892-15/People

_check_their_smartphones_85_times_a_day_(and_they_dont_even_know
_the.aspx.

10. Sue Klebold, *A Mother's Reckoning: Living in the Aftermath of Tragedy* (New York: Crown, 2016), 86.

11. "What Is DNA?" Genetics Home Reference, National Library of Medicine, National Institutes of Health, https://ghr.nlm.nih.gov/primer/basics/dna.

12. Elesha Coffman, "What Is the Origin of the Christian Fish Symbol?" *Christianity Today*, August 2008, http://www.christianitytoday.com/history /2008/august/what -is-origin-of-christian-fish-symbol.html.

13. Justin McCarthy, "Majority in U.S. Still Say Moral Values Getting Worse," Gallup, June 2, 2015, http://www.gallup.com/poll/183467/majority-say -moral-values-getting-worse.aspx.

14. Laura Beck, "17 Things You Need to Know about Gymnastics Star Gabby Douglas," August 8, 2016, Cosmopolitan.com, http://www.cosmopolitan. com/lifestyle/news/a62197/gabby-douglas-facts-gymnastics-olympics-2016/.

15. Darla Atlas, "The Real-Life Inspiration for *Miracles from Heaven* Opens Up about Her Life-Changing Experience: 'The Angel Winked at Me,'" *People*, March 16, 2016, http://people.com/celebrity/miracles-from-heavens -annabel-beam-on-her-real-life-experience/.

16. John A. A. Thompson, SUPERthrive website, http://www.superthrive.com/.

17. Dictionary.com, s.v. "edify."

18. Geoff MacDonald and Mark R. Leary, "Why Does Social Exclusion Hurt? The Relationship between Social and Physical Pain," *Psychological Bulletin*, 131, no. 2 (2005): 202–223.

19. "New mtvU and Associated Press Poll Shows How Stress, the Economy, and Other Factors Are Affecting College Students' Mental Health," *PR Newswire*, May 21, 2009, http://www.prnewswire.com/news-releases/new-mtvu --associated-press-poll-shows-how-stress-the-economy--other-factors-are -affecting-college-students-mental-health-61937242.html.

20. Sara Bareilles, "I Wanna Be like Me," iTunes bonus track from *The Blessed Unrest* © 2013.

If you're living a
PERFECT, *charmed* life . . .
well then, this book <u>isn't</u> for you.

ISBN 978-1-4143-7331-7 (Deluxe LeatherLike)

ISBN 978-1-4143-1938-4 (Softcover)

If, like the rest of us, you are at times broken, confused, lonely, or scared—if you're struggling with problems that you think "good Christians" don't have—then welcome, girlfriend, and pull up a chair! *The One Year Book of Inspiration for Girlfriends* is a quirky, friendly, and gut-honest devotional straight from the heart of Ellen Miller (CEO, marketing executive, mom, and un-apologetic "glorious mess"). There's no subject she's afraid to tackle! Her quick, daily doses of encouragement will make you laugh, give you something to look forward to, help you to stay (somewhat!) sane . . . and remind you that you're never alone.

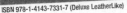